Leone Levi

International Law

With materials for a code of international law

Leone Levi

International Law
With materials for a code of international law

ISBN/EAN: 9783337233471

Printed in Europe, USA, Canada, Australia, Japan

Cover: Foto ©Suzi / pixelio.de

More available books at **www.hansebooks.com**

THE INTERNATIONAL SCIENTIFIC SERIES
VOLUME LX

THE INTERNATIONAL SCIENTIFIC SERIES

INTERNATIONAL LAW

WITH MATERIALS FOR A CODE OF INTERNATIONAL LAW

BY

LEONE LEVI, F. S. A., F. S. S.

OF LINCOLN'S INN, BARRISTER-AT-LAW
PROFESSOR OF COMMERCIAL LAW IN KING'S COLLEGE, LONDON
DOCTOR OF POLITICAL ECONOMY OF THE UNIVERSITY OF TÜBINGEN, ETC.

NEW YORK
D. APPLETON AND COMPANY
1888

THIS WORK IS, BY GRACIOUS PERMISSION,

DEDICATED TO

HER MAJESTY THE QUEEN

OF THE UNITED KINGDOM OF GREAT BRITAIN
AND IRELAND,

UNDER WHOSE ENLIGHTENED REIGN

INTERNATIONAL RELATIONS HAVE BEEN EXTENDED,

INTERNATIONAL ARBITRATION HAS RECEIVED

A POWERFUL SANCTION,

AND THE AUTHORITY OF INTERNATIONAL LAW HAS BEEN

MORE FULLY RECOGNIZED.

PREFACE.

I HAVE undertaken this work under the conviction that it would be of great advantage to reduce into the form of a Code the leading principles of the Law of Nations; that the greater diffusion of knowledge of such Law would often prevent disputes; and that, on the occurrence of differences between States, a collection of the well-established rules of the same would facilitate a resort to International arbitration, as the best method for securing just and equitable decisions consistent with the rights and dignity of States. The codification of International Law, in as far as it is in the power of a private writer to accomplish, has already been attempted by David Dudley Field and Bluntschli, but their works did not include the positive portion of the Law—that resulting from Treaties and Conventions. Yet these cover a large and ever-widening field, and determine the rights and duties, not only of States, but of subjects or citizens of the same, on many important civil and commercial relations, in time of peace and war. Especially useful, moreover, will be found the copious statements of the Treaties concluded between different States on the various subjects treated in the work, for which I am indebted to Martens' collection of Treaties. Though the need of keeping within certain limits has restrained me from making the work as exhaustive as I would have desired, and hindered my giving frequent and copious reference to the leading authorities, I trust that the materials now supplied for a Code will be found sufficiently full, lucid, and sequent.

LEONE LEVI.

5, Crown Office Row, Temple,
September, 1887.

CONTENTS.

---·◆·---

INTERNATIONAL LAW.

CHAPTER I.

CHAPTER II.

CHAPTER III.

MATERIALS FOR A CODE OF INTERNATIONAL LAW.

CHAPTER I.

CHAPTER II.

CHAPTER XXII.

CHAPTER XXIII.

CHAPTER XXIV.

CHAPTER XXV.

APPENDIX.

INTERNATIONAL LAW.

CHAPTER I.

NATURE AND AUTHORITY OF INTERNATIONAL LAW.

INTERNATIONAL LAW, or *Jus inter gentes*, is composed of two distinct elements, the Natural and the Conventional. The Natural, or what is designated as the Law of Nature, is common to all nations, for it embraces those principles which are implanted by God in the heart and mind of every man, of whatever race or clime. It is characterized, in a general sense, as a Law, because its observance leads to peace and happiness, and its disregard to war and misery. Unfortunately, however, natural or moral Laws impose only imperfect duties, and, therefore, in so far as International Law depends upon, and consists of the Law of Nature, it is of necessity of uncertain obligation. The Conventional, or positive element of International Law, is that which results from express obligations, undertaken by States in the shape of treaties, agreements, declarations, and

also from precedents and leading Cases, establishing
the customary practice of States. These two elements,
the Natural and the Conventional, are either inter-
mixed or separate. There may be a natural obligation, where there is not a conventional, though there
is scarcely a conventional obligation, without the
natural element bound up with it. But of the two
elements, the Natural, which is the most unchangeable
and universal, is also the less certain in its operation
and authority. Could we give to the universal principles of Natural Law the same certainty and binding
force as are possessed by the Conventional, we would
not have to lament—to the same extent, at any rate—
the weakness and uncertainty which characterize by
far the greatest portion of the Law of Nations.

We must not confound International Law with
politics, or the political system of a Nation. Political
Science is that part of social science which treats of
the principles of Government. In theory, it seeks to
establish Laws drawn from experience and reason,
sometimes as the generalized expression of facts, and
sometimes as the pure conception of an ideal more or
less realizable. In practice, it aims to give effect to
such general principles, with due regard to opportunity, time, place, and circumstances. The political
systems of States differ according to the character of
different races and peoples. The Orientals, by uniting
in one system theology and politics, create a theocratic *régime* hard and inflexible. Western nations,

less fettered, are better able to adapt their systems
of politics to the condition of Society.

International Law, as a branch of Jurisprudence,
is the creation of moralists, moulded by the acumen
of jurists and the wisdom of statesmen. What per-
plexed mediæval theologians was—Can a Christian
engage in war? To whom belongs the right of declaring war? What causes will justify a resort to
war? In a just war, what are the rights of Belligerents? Can a Christian make war against an
Infidel on no other ground but his infidelity? Has
the Pope the right to sanction war against an Infidel?
Can the Emperor sanction it, since he is not the
master of the world? Are we bound to keep faith
with the enemy? Jurists are not fond of hypothetical
questions, but they were early led to consider many
legal questions arising from the relations of States and
the rights of Embassies.

Grotius combined in a conspicuous manner the
character of a jurist and a theologian, and was able
to weigh with even hand the often conflicting rights
of morals and law. The spirit in which he entered
on his work, " De Jure Bellis et Pacis," * may be seen
from the opening statement. " I have been for a long
time convinced that there is a God common to all
Nations, who watches both the preparation and the
course of war. I have seen, on all sides, in the Christian World, such a wanton licence in war, that even

* Prelimin. Discourse, § xxix.

the most barbarous nations would have reason to blush for it. People run to arms without reason, or for the slightest reason, and they trample under foot all Divine and human laws, as if they were justified and resolved to commit all sorts of crimes without any check whatever." Are there no Laws, positive or natural, binding nations not to indulge in such barbarities? Grotius reviewed all the dicta and sayings of philosophers and moralists, consulted the practice of ancient and modern nations, examined the teaching of the Bible on matters of peace and war, and endeavoured to arrive at a kind of universal consensus on the subject, in the hope that no civilized State would feel itself at liberty to depart from the same.

The critical point in International Law, doubtless, is the lawfulness or unlawfulness of war, and it is unfortunate that the great authority of Grotius was not more decisively expressed against a system so fraught with misery and destruction. Who, indeed, can reflect on the sacredness of human life, in view of its eternal destinies, without coming to the conclusion that war, with its attendants, hatred, destruction, and slaughter, is incompatible with the high dictates of religion? It was not in vain, however, that Grotius wrote his splendid work. And the numerous writers who followed him in developing the principles of International Law have by their appeals to reason, conscience, and self-interest, for some restraint on the lust of power, done much to check lawlessness and barbarism, even in war. We may now say that the obligation of Treaties is better recognized; that the relations of States have become closer and more friendly; and that if war is still admitted as inevitable, under certain circumstances, it is certainly entered into with more hesitation, whilst every care is taken to circumscribe its limits as much as possible. We have, moreover, some security against a thoughtless recourse to war, in the fact that the leading States are bent upon promoting the economic welfare of their people, and the people themselves are better able to appreciate the great stake they have in the preservation of peace. What we grievously lament is the implicit trust placed on physical force, as a safeguard for the upholding of national rights. The maintenance of large military and naval forces is a disturbing element, which at any moment may place the reign of Law in great jeopardy.

Much has yet to be done before a sound system of public law, both internal and external, can be effectively established. No empire which exists by force can be said to have its public law founded on a solid basis. A low state of political education hinders the extension of a wise and beneficent constitutional system. If the public Law of Europe is ever to deserve the title of model and exemplar for all civilized nations, it must seek to unite the various branches of the family of States by bonds more solid and lasting than those of conquest; it must provide some other method than war for the settlement of international disputes; it must seek to harmonize the policy of States more with the maxims of philosophers and moralists, and with the precepts of religion and morals, than with the promptings of interest and expediency; it must seek to reverse the old maxim of "Nothing which is useful can be unjust" for the better one of "Nothing can be permanently useful which is unjust."

Jeremy Bentham indicated, as modes of preventing war, the homologation of unwritten laws, which are considered as established by custom, the conclusion of new conventions, and the settlement of new international laws, upon points which remain unascertained, and on which the interests of States are capable of collision. The materials offered in this work will, it is hoped, advance an object so desirable. Remove any uncertainty as to requirements of International Law, and reduce its principles in the form of a Code, if possible authoritatively recognized by all civilized states in the same manner as the "Declaration of Maritime Law" agreed to at the Congress of Paris of 1856, and the Geneva Convention for the amelioration of the condition of the wounded in armies in the field, in 1865; let the principles of International Law be made as accessible and intelligible as possible; let us have, in short, a clear, concise, and systematic Code of the Law of Nations, and we shall not only have taken an important step towards securing obedience to its dictates, but shall have greatly facilitated the labours of any Tribunal of Arbitration which may hereafter be organized for the settlement of international disputes.

LITERATURE OF INTERNATIONAL LAW.

The following are the principal works on International Law or the Law of Nations :—

1509–1566. Vasquez, "Controversiæ Illustres."
1588. Gentili, "De Jure Belli."
1619. Suarez, "De Legibus et Deo Legislatore."
1625. Grotius, "De Jure Belli et Pacis."
1650. Dr. Zouch, "Juris et Judicii Fecialis."
1672. Puffendorf, "De Jure Naturæ et Gentium."
1676. Rachel, "De Jure Naturæ et Gentium."
1688. Thomasius, "Institutiones Jurisprudentiæ Divinæ."
1693. Leibnitz, "Codex Juris Gentium Diplomaticus."
1737. Van Bynkershoek, "Quæstiones Juris Publici."
1748. Vattel, "Droit des Gens."
1749. Wolff, "Jus Gentium."
1754. Dr. Rutherforth, "Institutes of Natural Law."
1757. Hubner, "Essai sur l'Histoire du Droit Naturel."
1763. Burlamaqui, "Droit Naturel et Politique."
1778. Lampredi, "Juris Naturæ et Gentium."
1780. Moser, "Versuch des Neuesten Europaischen Volkerrechts."
1785. Martens, Geo. F., "Primæ Lineæ Juris Gentium Europæorum Pratici."
1795. Azuni, "Sistema Universale de Principii del Diritto Marittimo dell' Europa."
1795. Ward, "History of the Law of Nations."
1803. De Rayneval, "Institutions du Droit de la Nature et des Gens."
1819. Klüber, "Droit des Gens Moderne de l'Europe."
1836. Wheaton, "Elements of International Law."

1839. Manning, "Commentaries on the Law of Nations."
1844. Heffter, "Das Europäische Völkerrecht der Gegenwart."
1845. Gardner, "Institutes of International Law."
1847. Phillimore, "Commentaries on International Law."
1849. Wildman, "History of International Law."
1851. Reddie, "Inquiries in International Law."
1860. Pierantoni, "Progresso del Diritto Publico delle Genti."
1861. Halleck, "International Law."
1861. Twiss, "Law of Nations."
1869. Fiore, "Le Nouveau Droit International Public."
1869. Bluntschli, "Droit International codifié."
1870. Calvo, "Le Droit International."
1872. Field, Dudley, "Outline of an International Code."
1880. Hall, W. E., "International Law."
1882. Lorimer, "Institutes of the Law of Nations."
Martens, "Recueil des Principaux Traités d'Alliance, de Paix, de Trève, de Neutralité, de Commerce, de Limites, d'Échange, etc., conclus par les Puissances de l'Europe tant entre elles, qu'avec les Puissances et États dans d'autres Parties du Monde," 1761 to the present time, continued by Saalfeld, Murhard, Samwell, Hopf, and Stoerk Gœttingue.

The following treatises on special subjects may also be consulted :—

Neutrality—Gessner, "Le Droit des Neutres sur Mer." 1865.
    "   Hall, W. E., "Rights and Duties of Neutrals." 1874.
    "   Hautefeuille, "Des Droits et des Devoirs des Nations Neutres." 1848–9.
Private International Law—Westlake, "A Treatise on Private International Law." 1880.
Extradition—"Recueil renfermant in extenso tous les Traités conclus jusqu'à 1 Janviers, 1883, entre les Nations Civilisées," by Kirchner. 1883.
Foreign Judgments—Piggott's "The Law and Practice of the Courts of the United Kingdom relating to Foreign Judgments." 1881.
"Geneva Arbitration Case and Countercase between the United Kingdom and United States of America relating to the Alabama Claims." 1872.

CHAPTER II.

PROGRESS OF INTERNATIONAL RELATIONS.

§ 1. From Ancient Times to the Peace of Westphalia, 1648.

SCARCELY any comparison can be instituted between the present international relations and those which existed among the nations of antiquity, for in olden times States seldom came in contact with one another, except for hostile purposes. International Law, such as is now recognized, is the creation of comparatively recent years; the result of the combined influence of philosophy and ethics, religion and civilization, commerce and political economy, to say nothing of the action of accelerated means of communication, such as railways, steam packets, and electric telegraphs.

In Greece, the few writers on the duties of States towards one another were not jurists or statesmen, but philosophers and moralists, and their doctrines were laid down in too abstract a manner to influence

2

the action of their governments. Whilst Plato and Socrates, Epicurus and Zeno, were philosophizing on rules for the conduct of life, and exhibiting with much force and dignity the attractiveness of virtue, slavery was a recognized status among the people, foreigners were treated as enemies, and the customs of war were of the most barbarous character. Among Greek cities and states, a certain recognition of international justice was shown by the action of the Amphyctionic Council—an institution more religious than political, for the pacific adjustment of disputes. That Council had doubtless some influence in restraining the savagery of intestine wars, by binding its members not to destroy any of the Amphyctionic Towns, not to turn away their running waters, and not to commit theft in the Temple of Delhi, the common centre of the confederacy. But the authority of the Council was confined to the twelve nations of the Hellenic name, associated with the worship of Apollos at Delphi, and Demeter at Thermopylæ.

As in Greece, so in Rome, the ethics of Cicero and other writers were far in advance of the ethics of the nation. Cicero apologized for the use of force as a means of repelling aggression, just as we justify the punishment of crime for the purpose of repressing its excesses. In theory the Romans had, for a time at least, their fecial laws, and their *Collegium feedalium*, for the purpose of controlling the conduct of their armies towards other nations in time of war, and no war was declared unless permitted by the feciales. The Romans knew better than any other nation the action of the Law of Nature, that unwritten body of obligations which lies at the foundation of moral duties. The *jus gentium* was, to the Romans, the Law of Nature found in and applicable to all men and to all countries. But such theories did not permeate the sentiments of the nation, or control the action of the State. With them, every consideration was subordinate to the love of and thirst for conquest. Blinded by the desire for universal dominion, the Romans did not see that any International Law did or could exist, and if they apprehended its existence, they certainly did not acknowledge its authority, nor observe its doctrines.

With the introduction of Christianity in Rome, a high motive for more friendly and peaceful intercourse between nations was created, which ought to have acted as a powerful force among its followers. Recognizing no difference between men of different races, laying down principles of conduct altogether at variance with those held by the general community, it might have been expected that Christianity should have inaugurated a new code of international obligations, more obligatory than any suggested by ethics or philosophy. But though Christianity eventually became the religion of the State, its teaching had but little influence on the policy of the Empire. A few of the early Christians conspicuous for high morals, having at first made determined resistance to the custom of war, ended with acquiescing with it as a punishment of God; whilst rulers and people, as a whole, remained impervious to the teaching of a religion adopted more as a political force than as a rule of life.

In the dark era which followed the disruption of the Roman Empire, great part of the salutary effects produced by Roman Law and order disappeared; * nevertheless, other and more benign influences modified the asperities of the times. The Pope of Rome assumed, not without some success, the dignified position of International Arbitrator or Judge. The Councils of the Church, held from time to time, attended by the Sovereigns in person, or their Ambassadors, by the dignified clergy and other influential classes from many countries in Europe, exercised a beneficial influence on international relations. The Crusades organized, at the bidding of Urban II., in order to deliver the Holy Land from the dominion of the Turks, had the effect of making many people, heretofore quite segregated, come into contact with one another. Whilst Chivalry and Knighthood did much to discourage brutal ferocity in manners, and an increasing commerce taught nations to regard each other, not as natural enemies, but as alike dependent

---

* The Roman law did not absolutely lose its authority, even during the darkest time of the Middle Ages. The Basilica, prepared by order of the Emperor Basil; the Aniani Breviarium, promulgated by Alaric II. in Gaul; the Fuero de Juzgos, published by the Visigoths in Spain, and the Theodosian Code, were all founded upon the Roman Law. The usages of the Goths, Ostrogoths, and Visigoths were everywhere abandoned in favour of Roman jurisprudence.

on the right use of the resources wisely distributed by Providence over the surface of the earth.

In the Middle Ages the Mediterranean was the centre of European Commerce, and the Italian Republics had the trade of the East in their hands. Not yet in possession of direct communication by sea with India, Europe received at the hands of the Italians many of those articles which Egypt and Syria sent to minister to European taste and luxury. These articles were first carried by land, by the most indirect and circuitous routes, from the interior of India to Goa, from Goa to Aden; thence they were brought by the Italians by sea to the Mediterranean coasts and from Venice or Genoa, Marseilles or Barcelona, distributed through the chief marts of merchandise in Europe. But Commerce was exceedingly adventurous in those days, and as Hallam said, "When neither robbery nor private warfare was any longer tolerated, there remained that great common of mankind, the Sea, unclaimed by any king, so that the liberty of the sea was but another name for the security of the plunderers." We need not be surprised, therefore, in finding that the relative rights and duties of enemies and friends, or of Belligerents and Neutrals, were fully recognized and regulated by written customs.

The "Consulato del mare," a work which embodied the customs of the sea, variously given as issued between the twelfth and fourteenth century, gave

unequivocally its decision on one of the most interest-
ing questions of International Maritime Law,* viz.
Whether the property of a Belligerent found in a
neutral ship, and the property of a neutral found in a
Belligerent ship, were liable to confiscation. The rule
as laid down by the "Consulato" was as follows:—
"When an armed vessel meet a merchant Ship, and
both Ship and Cargo belong to the enemy, there is no
difficulty in deciding as to the course to be pursued.
The Admiral, or the chief of the force, is bound to
capture them both. But when the ship belongs to a
friendly state, and the goods to the enemy, then the
Admiral may compel the Master of the Ship to give up
the goods, on his paying the freight due to him upon
them. If, on the contrary, the Ship belongs to the
enemy, and the goods to friends, then the owner of the
Ship must agree with the Admiral for the redemption
of the Ship, at a reasonable price; and if they cannot
come to an agreement, then the Admiral has the right
to take the Ship to his own port, and the owner of the
goods is bound to pay freight upon the same, as if the
Admiral had taken the goods to the place of their
destination." And these are the principles which
Holland adopted in her war with the Hanseatic
League, and which were subsequently defended by
Grotius and other writers.

As trade passed from the Mediterranean to the

---

* "Consulato," ch. ccxxxi., "De nau de mercederia presa per nau
armada."

centre and north of Europe, the "Rôles d'Oléron," the "Guidon de la Mer," the "Laws of Wisbuy," the "Ordinances of the Hanseatic League," etc., extended further and further the laws and policy of the Mediterranean. And as intercourse became enlarged, both by land and sea, more especially by the discovery of America in 1492, and, the opening of a sea route to India in 1497, the anti-social spirit once prevailing gradually gave place to more peaceful and mutually helpful relations.

Important events, however, succeeded those magnificent discoveries. From that time dates the extension of the Colonial system, in which Portugal, Spain, Holland, and Great Britain won so many laurels. Soon after came the revolution of the Netherlands, and their rebellion from Spain, with the wars and alliances which their action called forth. And then came, too, the Reformation and the Thirty Years' War, which convulsed Europe to its very centre. The Peace of Prague of 1635 had been acceded to by the Elector of Brandenburg and other German Princes, but Sweden rejected it, and it was only after, in conjunction with France, she obtained a victory against the Emperor Ferdinand, that the Peace of Westphalia became possible. By that time the Holy Roman Empire, already on the wane, was infested by the incursion of the Turks in the south, and by insubordination in the north, an insubordination which not even the Golden Bull granted by the Emperor Charles

IV. had succeeded in quelling. England, then suffering under the reign of the Stuarts, was sending forth the Pilgrim Fathers to secure in the American soil that freedom of conscience which was denied to them at home. And France under Louis XIV., and Spain under Philip IV., were alike the seats of intolerance and despotism.

The Peace of Westphalia of 1648, including the Treaty of Münster, the Treaty of Osnabrück, and the Convention of Nuremberg, enlarged the basis of the political system of Europe, by the introduction for the first time of the Northern element in its affairs, by the recognition of the right of every State in Germany to be either Catholic or Protestant, as it might choose, and by the affirmation of the principle of equality among States, whether great or small, before International Law—a provision afterward rendered the more visible by the introduction of permanent embassies. But who were the signatories of these important Treaties? They were the Emperor of Austria, the Kings of France and Sweden, a number of Electors and Bishops, and the representatives of several free towns. England was no party to them. She had no voice in the political settlement of Europe in the seventeenth century. Russia did not then exist as a political power. Prussia figured only in her embryo condition as the Duchy of Brandenburg. Tested by results, the subversion of the unity of Germany, under the influence of religious animosities, proved a source of weakness, not of strength to Europe. The cession of Alsace to France * healed only for a time the sore between the two contiguous States, and only partially quelled the feuds which had existed between them ever since the Treaty of Verdun in 843.

§ 2. From the Peace of Westphalia to the Treaty of Vienna, 1815.

After the Treaty of Westphalia, new interests were created, as well as new combinations, and new complications in politics. The aim of France, under the dexterous guidance of Cardinals Richelieu and Mazarin, being to rival if not to excel in political influence the House of Austria, she found in the pretension of a right of succession to the Spanish Kingdom a chance of extending her territorial possessions. That there should be no Pyrennees was the aim of Louis XIV. in advancing the claim of Philip, Duke of Anjou, his Grandson, to the throne of Spain. But the aggrandizement of a Sovereign so absolute and intolerant could not fail to be regarded with jealousy by

---

* See "Acte de cession des trois évêchés de Lorraine, de Alsace, de Brisac, et de Pignerol, délivré à la France par l'Empereur et par l'Empire à Munster, le 24 Octobre, 1648;" "Acte de cession de la ville de Brisac, du Langraviat d'Alsace, et de la préfecture des dix villes impériale d'Alsace délivré à la France par l'Empereur et la maison d'Autriche." These districts included Metz, Toul, Verdun, as well as Strasburg and Bâle. "Traités, etc., la France et les puissances Étrangères, par Chr. Koch," 1802.

England, which was just emerging from the revolution of 1688; by Holland, which knew what Spanish terrorism had been to herself; by Prussia, which claimed to be the champion of Protestantism; and by Austria, which objected to any extension of French power. A League of these States was thus formed against France, and a war of thirteen years' duration ensued, which ended by the Treaty of Utrecht * of 1713.

The principle asserted by both the Treaties of Westphalia and Utrecht was the balance of power, or the maintenance of a kind of equipoise between States, with a view of resisting an inordinate increase of territory in the hands of any one State, and the uniting together of all States for their common interest in any measures necessary for preventing the same. But the very attempt to maintain such a balance of power produced greater evils than it intended to remove. Nor could it eliminate all the circumstances which might lead to the acquisition by any State of additional territories; for though the Treaty of Utrecht so far deterred the Sovereigns of Europe from attempting, by their own acts, to enlarge

---

* The Treaty of Utrecht was written in Latin and English, and was concluded by Princess Anne, Queen of Great Britain, France, and Ireland, and Prince Louis XIV., the Most Christian King, under date of Utrecht, $\frac{31}{11}$ day of $\frac{\text{March}}{\text{April}}$, 1713. It contains Letters Patent by the King admitting the renunciation of the King of Spain to the Crown of France, and those of M. the Duke of Berry and of M. the Duke of Orleans to the Crown of Spain. The Treaty is signed by a Public Notary and Writer and by other witnesses.

their sovereignty beyond the limits of their own
States, it could not prevent their obtaining accessions
of territories from *bonâ fide* hereditary rights. Thus,
after the death of Charles VI. of Austria, several
States claimed, as by right, certain territories, which
were alleged to have been bequeathed to Maria
Theresa, and that gave rise to another war of succession, settled by the Treaty of Tetschen * of May
13, 1779.

Experience also taught that, limit as we may the
right of succession, it will not prevent treaties of
alliance being concluded between contiguous States,
whereby physical boundaries may be set at nought.
In 1761, regardless of all that had been done to establish such a balance of power, a *pacte de famille* † was
concluded between Louis XV. in France and Charles
XII. of Spain, uniting all the members of the House
of Bourbon in a bond for their mutual protection.
Hence, when war arose between Great Britain and
France respecting the boundaries of their respective
colonies in North America, England found to her
surprise that her antagonist was not only France, but
Spain also; Charles VII. having, under that *pacte
de famille*, agreed to treat as enemy any Power which
should declare war against France, and also to guaran-

---

* At the Congress of Tetschen, Austria was represented by Count
de Cobenzell, Prussia by Baron de Riedésel, France as mediating
power by Baron de Bretenil, and Russia by Prince de Repnin.

† *Pacte de famille*—a treaty of friendship and union between the
Kings of France and Spain, signed at Paris, August 15, 1761.

tee to France all her possessions. The Treaty of Paris of February 10, 1763, between France, Great Britain, and Spain,* concluded after seven years' war, lessened the influence of France, lowered Spain to the position of a second-rate power, and placed British influence in North America in a condition of absolute safety.

After the conclusion of this Treaty, the distribution of power in Europe was greatly altered. Prussia, by the energy of her rulers, had become a kingdom of no mean importance. Russia, hitherto mainly composed of Asiatic tribes, became a European power. England had risen to the position of a great State. But again a source of disturbance appeared in the heart of Europe in consequence of the partition of Poland in 1772. And a revolution arose in the British colonies in North America of a formidable character, which ended in the creation in 1776 † of the United States of America. The war between Great Britain and her American

---

* The Treaty of Paris effected considerable transfers of territories. France ceded to Great Britain her possessions in Canada, Nova Scotia, and the islands on the St. Lawrence, French subjects being allowed to fish on the coast of Newfoundland. Great Britain ceded to France St. Pierre. The boundaries between France and Great Britain were fixed in the midst of the river Mississippi. Great Britain restored to France Guadeloupe and Martinique, and France ceded to Great Britain Grenada. Great Britain ceded to Spain Cuba, and Spain ceded to Great Britain Florida.

† In the month of July, 1775, a Confederacy was formed of "the thirteen United Colonies," and on July 4, 1776, the Congress issued a proclamation whereby they declared "the United States of America free and independent," with full power to levy war, conclude peace, contract alliances, establish commerce, and to do all other acts and things which independent States may of right do.

Colonies was the more prolonged and severe in consequence of the alliance contracted by France with the American Republic.* And it was during that conflict that Neutral Powers first assumed a firm attitude of resistance to belligerent rights.†

Hitherto France had been content to live under a feeble and retrograde Government. But the fermentation created by the extension of Jansenism, and the issue of the Bull *Unigenitus*; the agitation connected with the calling of the States-General; the alliance with Austria, formed by the marriage of the Dauphin with the Archduchess Marie Antoinette, and the disordered state of French finances, gave rise to a revolution in Paris in July, 1789, which became the immediate cause of a protracted European war. During the eventful time, which lasted from 1789 to 1814, the balance of power, so sedulously established by the Treaties of Westphalia and Utrecht, completely broke down; the old Republics of Holland, Venice, and Genoa

* "Traité d'amitié et de commerce entre le Roi de France et les Provinces Unies de l'Amerique à Paris, le 6 Février, 1778;" "Traité d'alliance eventuelle et defensive entre le Roi de France et les Provinces unies de l'Amerique à Paris, le 6 Février, 1778."

† On the question of neutral rights at that period, see Regulations of the King of France on neutral navigation in time of war, July 26, 1778; Declaration of the Empress of Russia, February 28, 1780; Declaration of Sweden to the Belligerent Powers, July 21, 1780; Maritime Convention between Russia and Denmark, July 7, 1780; Maritime Convention between Sweden and Russia, July 21, 1789, and between Prussia and Russia, May 8, 1781. See also the Earl of Liverpool's paper on the Contest of Great Britain in respect to Neutral Nations, 1785.

were destroyed, the Houses of Bourbon in Spain and
Naples were overthrown. And temporary Treaties
were concluded at Campo-Formio in 1797, at Luneville
in 1801, at Amiens in 1802,* at Presburg in 1805, at
Tilsit in 1807, and at Vienna in 1809, none of which
settled permanently any question of public Law.
Once again, Neutral States were exacerbated by the
operation of belligerents; the British Orders in Council
and the Decrees of Paris and Berlin being found exceedingly oppressive.   Irritated by the number of
American vessels captured by both parties, a war
ensued between Great Britain and the United States of
America, which was concluded by the Treaty of Ghent
of December 24, 1814. When the Congress of Vienna
assembled in 1815,† the map of Europe had in many
respects to be reconstructed.   Would that the people

* The Treaty of Amiens was signed March 27, 1802, by Joseph
Bonaparte for the French Republic, Lord Cornwallis for Great Britain,
the Chevalier d'Azara for Spain, and R. I. Schimmelpenninck for the
Batavian Republic.

† The Congress of Vienna was opened in 1814, and the con-
ferences were not suspended by the return to France of Napoleon in
March, 1815.   The final Act was signed July 9, 1815.   In that Con-
gress Austria was represented by the Prince of Metternich and the
Baron de Wissenberg; Spain, by Don Pierre Gomez de Labrador;
France, by the Prince de Talleyrand-Périgord, the Duke de Dalberg,
Comte de Latour du Pin, and the Comte Alexis de Noailles; Great
Britain, by the Viscount Castlereagh, Duke of Wellington, Earl of
Clancarty, Earl Cathcart, and Lord Stewart; Portugal and Brazil,
by the Comte de Palmella, Antoine de Saldanha de Gama, and Don
Joachim Lobo da Silveira; Prussia, by the Prince de Hardenberg
and Baron de Humboldt; Russia, by the Prince de Rasoumoffski,
Comte de Stackelberg, and Comte de Nesselrode; and Sweden and
Norway, by the Comte de Loewenhielm.

whose interests were so directly concerned had been in some manner consulted. The main desire, however, of the assembled representatives was to restore as far as possible the *status quo ante*, and to give compensations to the despoiled Sovereigns by dividing any available territory among them. By the Treaties concluded at Vienna in 1815, Malta was ceded to England, and Genoa to Sardinia. The Italian Peninsula was broken up into many little States, more or less under the influence of Austria. A German Confederation was formed. Sweden and Norway were united, as well as Holland and Belgium, each under one sovereignty. The Swiss Confederation was constituted, and the partition of Poland was confirmed, whilst the territory of France was reduced to its original dimensions.

The partition of Poland could not well be ignored by such a Congress, all the more that it had been regarded as a most flagrant violation of the sovereignty of States. Poland was, at all times, weak and powerless. With a people restless and turbulent, and her finances always in disorder, without a middle class, with a limited commerce, and with rulers ignorant and narrow minded, Poland had no element of stability within herself, to resist intrigues and opposition from within or from without. The Diet, in which any single member had a right, by his veto, to stop and nullify its proceedings, was at the mercy of any one who aimed at its subversion. It is not clear whether Maria Theresa of Austria, Catherine II. of Russia, or Frederick II. of Prussia was the first to propose the dismemberment of Poland; but overtures to this effect were made in 1770, and the act was consummated in 1772 * by the sudden invasion of the country by the allied troops of Russia, Prussia, and Austria. At the Congress of Vienna these Powers came to demand an official recognition of their act of spoliation, and they obtained it to the full. A new kingdom of Poland was indeed established, guaranteed by Russia, and Cracow was constituted a Republic, guaranteed by Austria; but in 1832 the kingdom of Poland became an integral part of the Russian Empire, and in 1846 Cracow was incorporated with Austria. At the conclusion of the Congress of Vienna, in September, 1815, Austria, Prussia, and Russia concluded a Holy Alliance, by which the three Sovereigns undertook to regulate their politics according to the dictates of religion. And to that Treaty, the accession of several other States was afterwards given.† The Prince Regent of Great Britain, however, refused to accede to the same, not so much on account of its

* The first dismemberment was made by Treaties between Austria and Russia; Prussia and Russia, July 25, 1772; the second dismemberment, by a declaration signed at St. Petersburg, between Austria and Russia, and by Treaty between Prussia and Russia in 1795.

† Among those who acceded to the Holy Alliance were the King of Saxony on May 2, 1817; Würtemburg, August 17, 1816; Switzerland, accepted by Russia on May 7; and by Prussia on September 10, 1817. The Hanseatic towns acceded to it in 1817; Sardinia, June 8, 1816; the Netherlands, September 26, 1815.

principles, as because the Treaty partook of the
character of a personal bond among the Sovereigns
themselves, whilst the British Constitution demanded
that any Treaty should be signed by a responsible
Minister.

§ 3. From the Congress of Vienna to the Present Time.

But such an alliance of the three Sovereigns did
not prevent a speedy outburst of popular indignation
in the States which were suffering from the harsh
and despotic rule imposed upon them. An occasion,
therefore, soon came to test the value of the compact
for mutual defence implied by the Holy Alliance. A
revolution having taken place at Naples in 1821, a
Conference was held at Laibach, a small town in
Austria, in which the three Powers were represented,
to consider what steps could be taken to suppress the
same. And a resolution was passed, establishing their
right of armed intervention in the affairs of any neighbouring States which might be troubled by faction,
a resolve which virtually gave a mandate to Austria to
go and crush the revolution in Naples and Sicily in
support of the Bourbon ruler. On the other hand,
and in a far different spirit, when, after years of cruel
oppression, the Greeks rose up in arms in 1826 to
shake off the yoke of Turkey, Great Britain, France,
and Russia agreed upon a pacific intervention for the

purpose of stopping the effusion of blood. And the result of their interference was a Treaty concluded in 1830, by which the kingdom of Greece was created, under the guarantee of the Powers. In that same year also, France, tired of the weak and retrograde Government imposed upon her by the Allied Powers, rebelled against Charles X., who represented the elder branch of the Bourbons, and elected to the throne Louis Philippe, the head of the younger branch of the same House, who ascended the throne with a constitutional charter in his hands. Simultaneously with the revolution in France, Belgium revolted against her union with Holland, and the kingdom of Belgium was constituted, under the guarantee of Great Britain, Austria, Prussia, and Russia.

The Greek rebellion suggests a brief digression on the arrival of the Turks in Europe, which became in time an important element in European history. Early in the Middle Ages, Constantinople was still the seat of the practically defunct Roman Empire; Greek Princes reigned in Epirus; Latin Principates were at Achaia and Morea; the Lusignans reigned in Cyprus; the Venetians were masters at Candia and Crete; the House of Anjou possessed Hungary, Sclavonia, Bosnia, Dalmatia, Croatia, and Servia; whilst Moldavia and Wallachia formed separate States. The conquest of Constantinople by Mohammed,* in

---

* The Koran proclaimed a holy war in the words, "Make war against those who do not believe in God. Fight with them, till they are converted, or till they submit by paying tribute" (Koran, ix. 29).

1453, produced great alarm and consternation among neighbouring States, and many wars were waged to arrest the progress of so dreaded an enemy. But the Treaty of Carlowitz between the Porte, Austria, Poland, Venice, and Russia, concluded in 1699, stemmed the Ottoman invasion, and from that time a complete change took place in the relations of the Turks with the Christians. Instead of being any longer agitated by fear of the Turks, the European States were able to consider how far they would tolerate the presence of the Turks in their midst.*

At one time, the Ottoman States thought it incompetent with the principles of Islamism to conclude any Treaties with Christian Princes. It was only an armistice or a Capitulation † that they were willing to grant to the Christian or the Infidel. But the

* Mohammed took Constantinople in 1453, and the rest of the Greek Peninsula in 1461 ; also Bosnia and Wallachia in 1463. Soliman II. took part of Hungary, Transylvania, and Sclavonia, Moldavia, and Rhode in 1522. Salem II. conquered Cyprus from the Venetians in 1570. Mohammed IV. conquered Candia in 1669. But the treaty of Carlowitz of 1699 took from Turkey all Hungary. That of Passarowitz took from her Temeswar and part of Servia. After 1734 the Porte lost Bakovina and Little Tartary ; from 1809 to 1812 she lost the provinces between the Dnieper and the Danube. In 1819 Turkey lost the Ionian Islands ; from 1820 to 1830 she lost part of Greece ; in 1829 part of Armenia, as well as Moldavia, and Wallachia, and Servia. In 1833 she lost Algiers. And in recent years, Bulgaria, Bosnia, Herzegovina, Egypt, and Cyprus are practically, if not theoretically, no longer under Turkish rule.

† Capitulations were letters of privileges and immunities granted by the Sultan, first to the French and afterwards to other Christian Sovereigns, which the Sultan could at any time withdraw or modify.

time came when the Turks felt themselves compelled
to relinquish their exclusiveness, and to come to terms
with their antagonists.   Thus, by the Treaty of
Koutschiowii Kaynardii, between Russia and the
Porte, in 1774, Turkey agreed to respect the independence of the Tartars in the Crimea, to receive
a Russian Minister, to protect the Christian religion ·
and Churches within the Turkish territory, to permit
the free navigation of the Black and White Seas to
Russian ships, and to recognize the title of Empress
of all the Russias.   With Prussia, also, the Porte
entered into Treaty obligations as early as 1761 ; so
with Spain in 1782, with Austria in 1790, and with
Great Britain in 1799.   Nevertheless, as late as 1804
Turkey did not recognize any Law of Nations.   She
did not consider herself bound by the same system
of public Laws on which other Nations in Europe
had so long acted.   And on their side, the European
States found in the established customs of the Turks,
their arrogance, and their principles of government,
an effectual barrier against all common action with
them.   Turkey, therefore, was not represented at the
Congress of Vienna in 1815, and she was not included
in the system of public Law then recognized.

Any extension of intercourse between Europe and
the Porte was further hindered by the fact that the
Sultan, as the successor of the Kalifate, deemed himself
the head of a theocratic Government ; that the Ulemas,
or Doctors of Ecclesiastical Law, held a spiritual

authority, often stronger than that of the civil rulers; and that the Janissaries, an armed force, exercised their rights with all the fervour of religious enthusiasm. In 1826 the Sultan dissolved the body of Janissaries, replaced it by a regular army, and issued an Hatti Sheriff conceding equal political and religious rights to all the subjects of the Empire, without distinction of religion or race. But any expectation of effective and permanent reforms was speedily disappointed. In truth, with the Koran as a political Code, with a Government ruling by force over conquered States, with finances in a chronic state of disorder, with agriculture oppressed by arbitrary taxation, and with commerce and industry · utterly paralyzed from want of capital and credit, to say nothing of the institution of polygamy, so offensive to the moral sentiment of Europe, in what manner could the Sultan expect effectually to remodel his States, or to command the respect and confidence of other nations?

Such was the condition of Turkey in 1854, when a paltry quarrel about the Holy Places in Jerusalem, between the Greek and Latin Churches, respectively upheld by Russia and France, led to a conflict in which the leading Powers became engaged. The real issues of the war were, not the respective claims of the two Churches, but whether Russian or Franco-British influence should preponderate over Turkey. The Western Powers succeeded in the contest, and by the Treaty of Paris of March 30, 1856,* for the first time in her history, Turkey was placed in a position of direct responsibility towards Europe; the Sublime Porte having been admitted to participate in the advantages of her public Law and System, on condition, however, that the Sultan would endeavour to ameliorate the state of his subjects, and would record his generous intentions towards the Christian population of the Empire. The Sultan agreed to communicate to the contracting parties the Firman which he would issue to that effect, but on the express understanding that such communication should not give to the Powers any right to interfere, either collectively or separately, in his relations with his subjects, nor in the internal administration of his Empire.

By the Treaty of 1856, Turkey accepted the provisions of the Congress of Vienna respecting the free navigation of rivers, and engaged to apply the same to the Danube and its mouths, the signatory Powers, including Turkey, declaring that this engagement should thenceforth form part of the public Law of Europe, and that they should take it under their guarantee. By a separate convention, the prohibition to admit ships of war of foreign Princes within the

* The signatures to the Treaty of Paris were—for the United Kingdom, the Earl of Clarendon and Lord Cowley; for Austria, Count Buol-Shauenstein and Baron Hübner; for France, Count Walewski and Baron Bourqueney; for Prussia, Baron de Manteuffel and Comte do Hatzfeldt; for Russia, Count Orloff and Baron de Brunnow; for Sardinia, Count de Cavour and the Marquis de Villa-Marina; and for Turkey, Aali Pasha and Mehemmed Djemil Bey.

Straits of the Dardanelles and the Bosphorus was confirmed, and the Black Sea was declared neutralized, Russia and Turkey engaging not to establish or maintain upon its coast any military maritime arsenals, and to limit the number of war vessels within the same. By a Tripartite Treaty, moreover, England, France, and Austria bound themselves to guarantee, jointly and severally, the independence and integrity of the Ottoman Empire, any infraction of the stipulation of the Treaty to be considered by the signatory Powers as *casus belli*.

More important, however, than any dealing with the maladministration of the Sultan, and the checking of Russian extension southward, were certain valuable principles which were put forth by the representatives of the leading European Powers in Congress assembled. By Article VIII. of the Treaty of Peace, it was laid down that " if there should arise between the Sublime Porte and one or more of the signing Powers, any misunderstanding which might endanger the maintenance of their relations, the Sublime Porte and each of such Powers, before having recourse to the use of force, shall afford the other Contracting Parties the opportunity of preventing such an extremity by means of their mediation." A wish was further expressed in a Protocol of the Congress, " that States between which any serious misunderstanding may arise should, before appealing to arms, have recourse, as far as circumstances might allow, to the good offices of a friendly Power." And by a declaration on International Maritime Law, signed by the Ministers of all the Powers represented at the Congress, and adhered to by many other States, the important principles were established: (1) that Privateering is and remains abolished: (2) that the neutral flag shall cover enemy's goods, with the exception of contraband of war; (3) that neutral goods, with the exception of contraband of war, shall not be liable to capture under enemy's flag; and (4) that blockades, in order to be binding, must be effective—that is to say, maintained by a force sufficient really to prevent access to the coast of the enemy.

Scarcely had the peace of Europe been re-established, when an event of far-reaching importance turned public attention to several Asiatic States. The commercial relations between the United Kingdom and China were carried on for a considerable time through the East India Company, by Agents who traded in China, not in the open market, but with the Co-hong Merchants licensed for that purpose. Two attempts were made—by Earl Macartney in 1794, and by Lord Amherst in 1806—to enter into direct communication with the Chinese Government, but they did not succeed. In 1833 the monopoly of the East India Company being ended, a Resident Commissioner or Superintendent of Trade was established at Canton. But difficulties arose, in consequence of the smuggling of opium into China by or with the connivance of

British traders from India, notwithstanding repeated proclamations by the Chinese Government against the same, which ended in war. By the Treaty of Nan-king of August 29, 1842, the adamantine walls which separated the Celestial Empire from the rest of the world were at last removed, and hopes were entertained that a better accord might thenceforth exist between the two Powers. But not many years after a quarrel arose respecting the opening of the Treaty ports, and the freedom and security of Christian missions, which caused another China war, in which France took part. By the Treaty of Tien-sing of June 26, 1858, all causes of contention were removed, and, as a pledge of more friendly and permanent relations between China and the Western Powers, provisions were made for the mutual maintenance of Embassies both at Peking and other capitals. Nor was the extension of political relations in the East allowed to be confined to China, for the Earl of Elgin, who conducted the negotiations with that country, proceeded forthwith to Japan, on an errand of peace. Already, in 1855, a Convention had been concluded by Sir James Sterling at Nagasaki, for regulating the admission of British ships in the ports of Japan; but the Earl of Elgin, by the Treaty of Yeddo, dated August, 1858, removed all obstacles in the way of regular relations between England and Japan, and provided for the maintenance of permanent Embassies in each other's kingdom.

3

Turning our attention from Asia to America, it was not without the deepest concern that, towards the end of 1860, Europe witnessed a serious insurrection in the United States—the Northern and Southern States being arrayed against each other, as in actual war. The insurrection ended with a restoration of the Union. But many were the questions of International Law thereby raised. The rebel States had formed themselves into a Confederation, representing a population of over 8,000,000, had established a Civil Government, had an army and were about constructing a navy. Was the Confederation a State capable of waging war with the United States, or were they only a people in rebellion? Did the fact of the two contending parties being practically, if not admittedly, at war, and the establishment of a blockade by the United States of the ports of the Confederate States, justify England and other States in granting belligerent rights to both sides? A British mail ship, having on board two diplomatic Agents of the Confederate States, on their way to Europe, was stopped by a United States cruiser, and the Agents were seized from the ship. Were they contraband of war? Is a mail ship a public ship? To what extent is the Government of a neutral State responsible for the sale or fitting out of war vessels for either belligerent by its subjects, after having cautioned them and taken care to execute the Laws in force relating thereto? The United States were at issue with the

United Kingdom on these and other difficult points which had arisen during the insurrection, and made heavy claims of compensation for losses alleged to have resulted to them from the neglect of duty on the part of Great Britain. But, happily, all these claims, under the name of the Alabama case, were referred for arbitration to a special tribunal, and amicably settled.

Returning again to events in Europe, we find France in 1848 changed from a Constitutional Monarchy into a Republic, and in 1852 from a Republic into an Empire. We find the Italian States, bent upon securing their independence, rallying round the constitutional State of Sardinia, and in 1859, with the aid of France, rescuing from Austria the Lombardo-Veneto provinces. After years of dissension, Hungary obtained an autonomous position from Austria, while Prussia became potent in North Germany. But the taking of the Schleswig-Holstein Duchies from the Crown of Denmark and their annexation to Germany aroused the jealousy of Austria, and so Prussia and Austria waged war with one another. By the Treaty of Prague of 1866, Austria relinquished Venice in favour of Italy, and Victor Emanuel was able to assume the title of "King of Italy." Yet once more the clatter of arms resounded in Europe. Jealous and wishing to arrest the extension of Prussian power, France, in 1870, opened a conflict which aroused an intense national feeling under a sense of danger, but with the complete success of German arms, a new German Empire was constituted in the great Hall of the Palace of Versailles, and France lost Alsace and Lorraine. With the fall of the Empire France became once more a Republic.

In the weakness of France, one of the parties to the Treaty of Paris of 1856, Russia, saw a favourable opportunity for asking to be released from the obligation she had then contracted of maintaining on the Black Sea only a limited number of war ships, and by her desire a Conference on the subject was held in London in 1871, when Russia, with the consent of all the Powers, and by the Trea y of May 13, 1871, was freed from her engagement. But again the condition of Turkey threatened the peace of Europe, the accounts of the sufferings of the Christians in Bulgaria and Bosnia having excited the strongest sympathies. In vain the European Powers appealed to the Sultan in favour of the Christian population in those States, and as the Conferences held on the subject proved fruitless, Russia made herself the champion of her co-religionists, and defeated the Turkish forces. The Russo-Turkish war ended by the Treaty of San Stefano. But a Congress assembled in Berlin, and by the Treaty of July 13, 1878,* Bulgaria was constituted

* The signatories to the Treaty of Berlin were—for the United Kingdom, the Earl of Beaconsfield, the Marquis of Salisbury, and Lord Odo Russell; for Germany, Prince Bismarck, B. de Bülow, and Prince Hohenlohe Schillingsfürst; for Austria, Count Andrassi, Count Cárolyi, and Baron de Haimerle; for France, M. Waddington, Count de Saint Vallier, and M. Desprez; for Italy, Count Corte and Count de Launay; for Russia, Prince Gortchakow, Count de Schouvaloff, and Paul d'Oubril; for Turkey, Caratheodory Pasha, Mehemed Ali Pasha, and Sadoullah Bey.

an autonomous and tributary Principality, Montenegro was declared free, and Servia and Roumania were made independent. But something more was done previous to this, for by a separate convention of defensive alliance between Great Britain and Turkey, signed June 4, 1878, Great Britain engaged to defend the territories of the Sultan in Asia, on his promise to introduce necessary reforms therein. And the Sultan consented to assign the island of Cyprus to be occupied and administered by England. Still later events in Egypt and Bulgaria are keeping the eyes of Europe with great tension directed to the fortunes of the Turkish Empire, and we are witnessing the gradual surrender by the once-dreaded Mussulman Power of many portions of her European territory.

Brief as is the survey thus made, it exhibits a considerable progress in international relations. Not only is there a large increase in the number of recognized States, but a higher conception is being formed of the rights and duties which bind them one to another. There is a closer relation between the different Governments by means of permanent embassies and consulates, and there is more commingling of their peoples by the increase of trade and communication. Everywhere there is an earnest desire to improve the condition of the masses of the people and to extend and develop the resources of States.

CHAPTER III.

THE POLITICAL CONDITION OF STATES.

EUROPE.

Austria-Hungary.

			Area. Eng. sq. miles.		Population, 1880.
Austria	...	...	116,000	......	22,144,000
Hungary	...	...	124,000	......	15,338,000
			240,000		37,482,000
Bosnia and Herzegovina			1,970	......	1,336,000
			241,970		38,818,000

Austria-Hungary is a Constitutional Monarchy. By a diploma of October 20, 1860, and a patent of February 26, 1861, the Constitutions previously in force in Hungary, Croatia, Slavonia, and Transylvania were restored, and a fundamental Law was passed for the establishment of the Reischrath or Imperial Council. In 1866 Hungary was allowed self-government by a responsible Ministry, with a delegation for the transaction of the joint business of the two halves of the Empire. On November 14, 1868, the name of Austria-Hungary was adopted.

The frontiers between Austria and Italy were settled or affected by the Treaty between Austria, France, and Sardinia of June 16, 1860, by the Treaty between Austria and Prussia of August 27, 1866, and by the Treaty between Austria and Italy of December 7, 1871.

Austria is party to the Treaty for the separation of Holland and Belgium of April 19, 1839; the pacification of the Levant of July 15, 1840; the navigation of the Dardanelles and Bosphorus of July 15, 1840; the succession to the Crown of Denmark of March 8, 1852; for guaranteeing the integrity and independence of the Ottoman Empire of April 15, 1856; the pacification of Syria of September 5, 1850; the navigation of the Black Sea and Danube, March 13, 1871; the Berlin Treaty for the Affairs of the East of July 13, 1878; the Navigation of the Danube of March 10, 1883; and the Act for the freedom of trade in the States of the Congo of February 26, 1885.

Belgium.

Area. Eng. sq. miles.	Population, Dec., 1845.
11,370	5,853,000

Belgium is a Constitutional Monarchy. By the Treaty of London of November 15, 1831, between Austria, Belgium, England, France, and Russia, Belgium, within the limits thereby fixed, was constituted an independent and perpetually neutral State, and bound to observe this neutrality with regard to other States. The territory was made to comprise the provinces of South Brabant, Liège, Namur, Hainault, West Flanders, East Flanders,

Antwerp, and Limbourg, and some part of the Grand Duchy of Luxembourg. By another Treaty, signed at London April 19, 1839, between the same States, and including the Netherlands, the Union which existed between Holland and Belgium in virtue of the Treaty of Vienna of May 31, 1815, was acknowledged by the King of the Netherlands as dissolved. It was again specified that Belgium, separated from Holland and formed into an independent State under the auspices of the Courts of Great Britain, Austria, France, Prussia, and Russia, should, within the limits specified in the Treaty, be an independent and perpetually neutral State, and made bound to observe such neutrality towards all other States. By a Treaty between Great Britain, Austria, Belgium, France, Italy, the Netherlands, Prussia, and Russia, signed at London May 11, 1867, the Grand Duchy of Luxembourg was declared to be neutralized, the high contracting parties engaging to respect the principle of neutrality so stipulated. That principle was placed under the sanction of the collective guarantee of the Powers signing parties to the Treaty, with the exception of Belgium, itself a neutral State. By a Treaty between Great Britain and Russia, signed in London August 9, 1870, Prussia engaged to respect the neutrality of Belgium during her hostilities with France, so long as the same should be respected by France. A Treaty to the same effect, and of the same date, was also concluded between Great Britain and

France, Great Britain agreeing to co-operate with either Power against the other, in order to insure the observance of such obligation.

In February, 1881, the International Association of the Congo was founded by the King of the Belgians,* for the purpose of promoting the civilization and commerce of Africa, and for other humane and benevolent purposes. Belgium is a party to the General Act of the Conference of Berlin, signed February 26, 1885, for the purpose of regulating the conditions most favourable to the development of trade and navigation in certain regions of Africa, and for securing to all nations the advantages of free navigation on the two chief rivers of Africa.

Denmark.

	Area. Eng. sq. miles.		Population, 1880.
Denmark	14,784	......	1,969,000
Possessions	75,106	......	127,000
	89,890		2,096,000

Denmark, a Constitutional Monarchy, once a Kingdom of considerable extent, now comprises the

* On September 12, 1876, a Conference was held at the Royal Palace at Brussels, on the exploration and civilization of Africa, and in 1877 au African Exploration Fund was established. The Comité d'Études was afterwards expanded into the "Association Internationale du Congo." By a decision of the Chamber of Representatives and Senate of Belgium, dated $\frac{28}{30}$ April, 1885, the King of the Belgians was authorized to be the chief of the State so founded, the union between Belgium and the new State of the Congo being exclusively personal.

Peninsula of Jutland on the European Continent, and a group of Islands in the Baltic. Norway, which had belonged to the Crown of Denmark since 1587, was ceded to Sweden in 1814. By the Treaties of August 1 and October 30, 1864, Denmark renounced all claims to Lauenburg, Holstein, and Schleswig. These were incorporated with Prussia, and now they form part of the German Empire.

France.

			Area. Eng. sq. miles.		Population, 1881.
France...	...	...	204,000	......	37,672,000
Possessions	...	...	1,125,000	......	27,723,000
			1,329,000		65,395,000

France, after having been for a considerable time a Kingdom under the elder branch of the Bourbon family, was declared a Republic on September 21, 1792. On May 18, 1804, Napoleon I. was, by a Senatus-Consulte, proclaimed Emperor of the French, and France continued an Empire till the peace of 1814. At the Restoration in 1815, after the Congress of Vienna, Louis XVIII., heir of the House of Bourbon, became King of France, and he was succeeded in 1824 by Charles X. But on August 3, 1830, after the revolution of July, Louis Philippe, the representative of the younger branch of the Bourbon family, was elected King of the French. In February, 1848, another revolution occurred, and once more France was declared a Republic, Louis Napoleon being chosen as President. On December 2, 1852, Louis Napoleon restored the Empire, and this lasted till September 4, 1870, when again France was declared a Republic. In 1830 Algiers became a French Colony. The frontiers between France and Germany were settled by the Treaty of September 14, 1871, and between France and Italy by the Treaty of February, 1860, upon the incorporation of Savoy and Nice with France. France is party to the Treaty for the Separation of Holland and Belgium of April 19, 1839; the navigation of the Dardanelles and Bosphorus, July 13, 1841; the succession to the Crown of Denmark, May 8, 1852; the succession to the Throne of Greece, November 20, 1852; the Treaty of Peace with Russia of March 30, 1856; the pacification of Syria of September 5, 1860; the neutralization of the Grand Duchy of Luxembourg of May 11, 1867; the revision of Stipulations on the Navigation of the Black Sea and Danube of March 8, 1821; the Berlin Treaty on the Affairs of the East of 1878; the Navigation of the Danube, March 10, 1883; and the Act on the Congo of February 26, 1885.

Germany.

Area. Eng sq. miles. 208,670	Population, December 1, 1885. 46,844,926

The following territories are under the protection of Germany, but no information exists of their exact area and population, viz.:

The territory of Togo on the coast of Africa, with the ports of Lomi and Bagidah.

Guinea Now, by the right of the river Rey, near Old Calabar and Cross rivers.

On the West Coast of Africa Cape Frio and Orange River.

The territory of the Negro Chiefs of Usagara, Ngourun, Onsegonha, and Oukami.

On the Ocean the Land of Emperor William, New Guinea.

The Congress of Vienna of 1815 formed the "German Confederation," which included the Sovereign Princes and the Free Towns of Germany, the Emperor of Austria, the King of Prussia, the King of Denmark for the Duchy of Holstein, and the King of the Netherlands for the Grand Duchy of Luxembourg. The federative Diet was to be presided over by Austria; it was to sit at Frankfort-on-Main, and the votes were distributed according to the relative influence of the various Members. On February 14, 1867, the North German Confederation was constituted, under the presidency of the King of Prussia; and on January 18, 1870, the King of Prussia was proclaimed Emperor of Germany. On April 16, 1871, by an alliance between the King of Prussia, in the name of the North German Confederation, the King of Bavaria, the King of Würtemburg, the Grand Duke of Baden, and the Grand Duke of Hesse, the German Empire was formed; and by this Act Germany has succeeded to all the rights and obligations of Prussia and other German States.

The frontiers between France and Germany were settled by the Treaties of September 14, 1871, and March 20, 1872, and by them Alsace and Lorraine, which had been possessed by France since 1713, were restored to Germany. In consequence of the protectorate assumed by Germany over portions of the African coasts, an arrangement was entered into between Great Britain and Germany relative to their respective sphere of action in those territories in June, 1885 ; also as regards the Gulf of Guinea in September, 1886 ; and respecting the Western Regions in the Western Pacific on April 6, 1886.

Great Britain and Ireland.

	Area. Eng. sq. miles.		Population, 1881.
United Kingdom	121,483	......	35,241,000
India and Ceylon	935,777	......	204,670,000
Dominion of Canada ...	3,406,542	......	4,325,000
Australasia	3,083,410	......	3,462,000
Other Colonies	1,428,138	......	62,494,000
	8,975,380		310,192,000

The United Kingdom of Great Britain and Ireland is formed by the Treaty of Union between England and Scotland of May 1, 1707, and by the Union of Great Britain with Ireland on January 1, 1801. The succession of the British Crown was settled by the 12 and 13 Will. III. c. 2 to the Princess Sophia of Hanover and the heirs of her body being Protestants. The British Colonies are of three classes : 1st, Crown Colonies, in which the Crown has the entire control of legislation, the administration being carried on by public officers, under the control of the Home Government ; 2nd, Colonies possessing representative Institutions, but not responsible Government, in which the Crown has no more than a veto on Legislation, the Home Government retaining the control of public officers; and 3rd, Colonies possessing representative institutions and responsible Government, in which the Crown has only a veto on legislation, and the Home Government has no control over any officer except the Governor. The Government of India was transferred by the East India Company to the Crown in 1858, by the 21 and 22 Vict. c. 106.

Great Britain is party to the Treaties for the separation of Holland and Belgium, April 19, 1839; the Pacification of the Levant, July 15, 1840; the closing of the Dardanelles and Bosphorus, July 13, 1841; the succession to the Crown of Denmark, May 8, 1852; the succession to the throne of Greece, November 20, 1852; the Treaty of Peace of March 30, 1856; the integrity and independence of the Ottoman Empire of April 15, 1856; the pacification of Syria of September 5, 1860; the neutralization of Luxembourg of March 11, 1867; the independence and Neutrality of Belgium of April 9, 1870; the revision of the Treaty of Peace of March 13, 1871; the Berlin Treaty of July 13, 1878; the Treaty for the Navigation of the Danube of March 10, 1883; and the Treaties respecting the Congo of 1885.

Greece.

Area. Eng. sq. miles. 24,969	Population, 1879. 1,979,561

In 1821, a revolution having occurred at Patras, a meeting was held at Argos to organize a provisional Government, and on January 27, 1822, at a Congress assembled at Piræus, the independence of the Greek nation was formally declared. On July 6, 1827, France, Great Britain, and Russia signed a Treaty for the pacification of Greece, but the same having left Greece under the suzerainty of Turkey, it failed to satisfy the desire of the people. In 1832, by a Convention, dated May 7, between France, Great Britain, Russia, and Bavaria, Greece, under the guarantee of the three Courts of Great Britain, France, and Russia, was constituted into a monarchical and independent State. By the Treaty of November 14, 1863, between France, Great Britain, and Russia on the one part, and the King of the Hellenes on the other part, the Ionian Islands, which by the Congress of Vienna were placed under the protection of the United Kingdom, were united with the Hellenic Kingdom. And by the Treaty of May 24, 1881, the territory of Greece was further enlarged, and the frontiers between Greece and Turkey newly settled.

Holland.

	Area. Eng. sq. miles.		Population, Dec. 31, 1835.
Holland	12,137	......	4,336,000
Possessions	50,952	......	20,630,000
	63,089		24,966,000

By the Treaty of Vienna of June 9, 1815, the ancient United Provinces of the Netherlands and the theretofore Belgian Provinces were united under the sovereignty of the Prince of Orange-Nassau. A revolution having taken place in Brussels in 1830, Austria, France, Great Britain, Prussia, and Russia, on November 15, 1831, entered into a convention for the constitution of a separate kingdom of the Belgian territory. And by the Treaty of April 19, 1839, between Austria, France, Great Britain, Prussia, and Russia on the one part, and the Netherlands on the other, the separation of Belgium was completed, and the Grand Duchy of Luxembourg united to Belgium. The fundamental Law of the Netherlands was promulgated November 3, 1848. Holland possesses Colonies in Java and Madura in the East Indies, Sumatra, Celebes, parts of Borneo and New Guinea, and Surinam and Curaçao in the West Indies.

Italy.

Area. Eng. sq. miles.	Population, Dec. 31, 1845.
114,380	29,699,785

Some possessions on the coast of the Red Sea.

The formation of the Kingdom of Italy was promulgated on March 17, 1861, when the constitution of Sardinia of March 4, 1848, was extended to the whole country. By the Treaty of June 10, 1860, between Austria, France, and Sardinia, Lombardy was incorporated with the kingdom. By the Treaty of Prague of August 27 and October 3, 1866, between Austria and Prussia, Venetia was ceded by Austria to Prussia, and by her to Italy. And in 1870, on the departure of the French army of occupation, Italy took possession of Rome, and constituted it the capital of the Kingdom.

By a Law passed on May 13, 1871, signed by Victor Emmanuel, King of Italy, and all his Ministers, the relations between the Pope and the Italian Government were settled as follows :—

1. The person of the Sovereign Pontiff is sacred and inviolable.

2. An attempt against the person of the Sovereign Pontiff is to be punished in the same manner as an attempt against the person of the King.

3. The discussion on religious subjects is free.

4. The Italian Government renders to the Sovereign Pontiff in the territory of the Kingdom sovereign honours.

5. A dotation is settled in favour of the Holy See of the amount of 3,225,000 lires in *rentes annuelles* free of taxes.

6. The Sovereign Pontiff will enjoy the Apostolic Palaces of the Vatican and Lateran, such Palaces, Villas, Museums, Libraries, Art collections, etc., being inalienable.

7. The Sovereign Pontiff is free to fulfil all his functions.

8. The Envoyés of foreign Governments to His Holiness will enjoy all the prerogatives and immunities which belong to diplomatic Agents, according to International Law.

9. The Sovereign Pontiff corresponds freely with the Episcopate in the whole Catholic World.

10. In matters spiritual and disciplinary no complaint or appeal is admitted against the acts of the Ecclesiastical Authorities, but no executive force is given to such acts. Such acts have no effect if they are contrary to the Law of the State or public order, or if they do wrong to the rights of private persons, and they are subject to the Penal Law if they constitute a crime.

Italy has succeeded to all the rights and obligations of the former Kings and Princes of the Italian States. She is party to the Treaty for the neutralization of the Grand Duchy of Luxembourg of March 11, 1847; the revision of certain stipulations of the Treaty of March 30, 1856, by the Treaty of May 13, 1871; the

Berlin Treaty of July 13, 1878; the Treaty for the Navigation of the Danube of March 10, 1883; and the Act for the Trade of the Congo of 1885.

Portugal.

	Area. Eng. sq. miles.		Population, 1881.
Portugal	35,541	......	4,708.000
Possessions	704,150	......	4,984,000
	739,991		9,692,000

The fundamental Law of Portugal is the Carta de Ley, granted in 1826 by Dom Pedro IV., and revised by the Cortes in 1852. By a Treaty signed at Lisbon May 16, 1703, Great Britain and Holland agreed to defend Portugal against Spain and France, should either of them, or both together, make war against her.

Roumania.

Area. Eng. sq. miles. 50,159	Estimated population. 5,576,000

By the Treaty of Paris of 1856, the Principalities of Moldavia and Wallachia were placed under the collective guarantee of the contracting Powers, whilst remaining under the suzerainty of the Porte. In 1857 the Union of the two Principalities was proclaimed, under the name of Roumania. By a Convention between Austria, France, Great Britain, Prussia, Russia, Sardinia, and Turkey, of August 19, 1858, the organization of the Principalities was established. In 1878, by the Treaty of Berlin, Roumania was recognized as an independent Kingdom, subject to the proviso that all its inhabitants should enjoy complete religious freedom. The fundamental Law of Roumania is the constitution of 1866.

Russia.

	Area. Eng. sq. miles.		Population, 1884.
Russia and Finland	1,750,659	......	87,472,000
Caucasus ...	182,449	......	2,176,000
Trans-Caspian ...	285,833	......	710,000
Central Asia ...	1,165,000	......	5,101,000
Siberia... ...	467,000	......	4,093,000
	3,850,941		99,552,000

Russia, originally limited to the Principality of Moscow, has by constant acquisitions extended its frontiers from the Baltic to the Black Sea in Europe, and in Asia as far as the Pacific eastwards, and to the borders of China southward. *

Russia is party to the Treaties for the separation of Holland and Belgium of April 19, 1839; the pacification of the Levant of July 15, 1840; the closing of the Dardanelles and the Bosphorus of July 13, 1841; the succession to the Crown of Denmark of May 8, 1852, and to the Throne of Greece of November 22, 1852; the Treaty of Peace of Paris, March 30, 1856; the pacification of Syria of September 5, 1860; the neutralization of Luxembourg of May 11, 1867; the

* The Sovereigns of Russia were named Autocratores, Magni Domini, Grand Princes, Czars or Tzars. Peter the Great first used the title of Emperor in 1721.

revision of the Treaty of Paris of March 13, 1871; the Berlin Treaty of July 13, 1878; and the Congo Treaty of 1885.

Servia.

Area. Eng. sq. miles.	Population, December, 1884.
18,781	1,903,000

The Principality of Servia was declared independent by the Treaty of Berlin of 1878, subject to the condition of maintaining perfect religious freedom.

For matters concerning Servia see Treaty of Peace between Russia and Turkey, Bucharest, $\frac{16}{28}$ May, 1812; Convention between Russia and Turkey, explanatory of Treaty of Bucharest, Ackerman, $\frac{7 \text{ October}}{25 \text{ September}}$, 1826; separate Act relating to Servia, annexed thereto, same date; Treaty of Peace between Russia and Turkey, signed at Adrianople September $\frac{2}{14}$, 1829; Hatti Sheriffs issued by the Sublime Porte to Servia, 1829, 1830, and 1833; Firman from the Sultan in December, 1838.

Spain.

	Area. Eng. sq. miles.		Population, 1884.
Spain	165,640	......	8,025,500
Possessions ...	194,756	......	17,268,600
	360,396		25,294,100

Spain was represented at the Congress of Vienna in 1815, but her territory had not been affected by the events which led to the same. Spain is governed by the Constitution of June 30, 1876. The sovereignty of Spain over the Caroline and Pelew Islands was recognized by Germany and Great Britain in 1886, in return for the grant of concessions touching trade, shipping, and the acquisition of land. The fortress of Gibraltar, at the extreme South of Spain, on the Mediterranean, was taken from Spain by England in 1704, and the Peace of Utrecht, in 1713, secured its possession to Great Britain.

Sweden and Norway.

			Area. Eng. sq. miles.		Population, Dec. 31, 1886.
Sweden	...	...	173,921	......	4,682,769
Norway	...	...	125,613	......	1,806,900
			299,534		6,489,669

The Union of Sweden and Norway, under the same King, was accepted by the Starthing, November 4, 1809. By the Treaty of peace between Denmark and Sweden, January 14, 1814, Denmark ceded to Sweden the Kingdom of Norway. The fundamental Law of the Kingdom dates from 1809.

By a Treaty between France, Great Britain, and Sweden and Norway, dated November 17, 1855, France and Great Britain, upon the undertaking of the King of Sweden and Norway not to cede to nor to exchange with Russia, nor to permit her to occupy, any part of the territories belonging to the Crown of Sweden and Norway, agreed to assist the King of Sweden with sufficient forces to resist any pretensions or aggressions of Russia.

Switzerland.

Area. Eng. sq. miles. 15,957	Population, December 1, 1880. 2,846,000

On August 16, 1814, an alliance was concluded between the nineteen Cantons, viz. Zürich, Berne, Lucerne, Uri, Schweitz, Unterwalden, Glaris, Zug, Fribourg, Soleure, Bâle, Schaffhausen, Appenzell, Saint-Gall, Grisons, Argovie, Thurgovie, Tessin, and Vaud, for the preservation of their freedom and independence. And by an act of acknowledgment and guarantee, dated Paris, November, 1815, Austria, France, Great Britain, Prussia, and Russia guaranteed to that country the integrity and inviolability of its territory. The Powers also acknowledged "that the neutrality and inviolability of Switzerland, and her independence of all foreign influence, enter into the true interests of the policy of the whole of Europe."

By Treaty of May 26, 1857, the Canton of Neuchâtel, formerly in possession of Prussia, was incorporated with Switzerland. A federal constitution for the Confederation was proclaimed May 29, 1874. The Legislative body of the Confederation is the Federal Assembly, which, besides its legislative functions, has the exclusive power to conclude Treaties, etc., declaring war and signing peace.

Turkey.

				Area. Eng. sq. miles.		Estimated population.
Europe	...	...	...	63,879	......	4,500,000
Asia	...	...	...	729,721	......	16,174,000
Africa	...	...	...	792,844	......	7,817,000
				1,586,114		28,491,000
Eastern Roumelia, autono- mous	...	...	...	13,857	......	975,000
Bosnia, Herzegovina, occu- pied by Austria	...	...	23,571	......	1,404,000
				1,623,872		30,870,000

The Turkish Empire comprises certain territories in its immediate possession in Europe, Asia, and Africa, and other territories belonging to Tributary States. The States immediately belonging to the Empire include within them Mussulman subjects and non-Mussulman subjects or Rajas, and Francs, viz. subjects of foreign Powers domiciled in Turkey. Turkey was admitted to the participation of the advantages of public Law, and of the European Concert, by the Treaty of Paris of March 30, 1856, on certain conditions therein expressed. By a Convention between Great Britain, Austria, and France, signed at Paris, April 15, 1856, these Powers guaranteed, jointly and severally, the independence and integrity of the Ottoman Empire, as recorded in the Treaty concluded at Paris on March 14, 1856. The Treaties of March 13, 1871, modifying the Treaty of Peace of March 30, 1856, modified the obligations contracted by the Porte as regards the Dardanelles and the Black Sea. By the Treaty of

Berlin the relations of the Porte to Bulgaria, Bosnia, Montenegro, Servia, and Roumania were altered. She undertook to maintain the principle of religious liberty. And by a Convention between Great Britain and Turkey of June 4, 1878, Great Britain undertook to defend the Turkish territory in Asia Minor; Turkey consenting to assign the island of Cyprus, to be occupied and administered by England.

Turkey was declared a Constitutional Monarchy on December 28, 1876.*

* Upon the navigation of the Black Sea, Dardanelles, and Bosphorus, see the following Treaties, Conventions, etc. :—

January 5, 1809. Treaty—Great Britain and Turkey. Straits closed to ships of war of foreign States when the Porte is at peace.

1822. Notification—Turkey. Bosphorus closed to merchant ships of Powers not having Treaties.

October 7, 1826. Treaty—Russia and Turkey. Trade to be opened to all friendly Powers.

September 14, 1829. Treaty—Russia and Turkey. Black Sea and Straits opened to merchant vessels of Russia, and to those of all Powers at peace with the Porte.

July 15, 1840. Convention—Great Britain, Austria, Prussia, Russia, and Turkey. Dardanelles and Bosphorus closed to foreign ships of war when the Porte is at peace.

May 3, 1841. Convention—Great Britain, Austria, France, Prussia, Russia, and Turkey. Dardanelles and Bosphorus closed to foreign ships of war when the Porte is at peace ; Firman for light vessels of war for service of missions.

December 24, 1844. Regulation—Turkey. Protection of Dardanelles and Bosphorus as to passage of sailing vessels and steamers through the Straits between sunset and sunrise.

March 30, 1856. General Treaty—Great Britain, Austria, France, Prussia, Russia, Sardinia, and Turkey. Limitation of Russian and Turkish naval forces; non-establishment of military-maritime arsenals.

March 13, 1871. Treaty—Great Britain, Austria, France, Prussia,

4

Bulgaria.

Area. Eng. sq. miles. 24,693	Population, 1881. 2,007,000

Bulgaria was, by the Treaty of Berlin of 1878, constituted an autonomous and tributary Principality, under the suzerainty of the Sultan. A province was also formed south of the Balkans, which took the name of Eastern Roumelia, and remains under the direct political and military authority of the Sultan under conditions of administrative autonomy, and that it be governed by a Christian Governor-general.

ASIA.

China.

	Area. Eng. sq. miles.		Estimated population.
China proper ...	1,554,000	......	382,000.000
Dependencies ...	2,914,000	......	21,000,000
	4,168,000		403,000,000

The relations of Great Britain with China are regulated by the Treaty of Nan-king of 1842, and the Treaty of Tien-tsin of June 26, 1858. An agreement was also concluded between the two Powers at Che-foo on September 13, 1876, ratified at London May 16, 1886, which settled further the condition of inter-

Italy, Russia, and Turkey. Abrogation of Treaty of March 30, 1886, respecting non-limitation of forces and establishment of arsenals.

Russia and Turkey. Same.

course between high officers in the capitals and the provinces, and between Consular officers and Chinese officials at the ports. It also laid down regulations for the conduct of judicial proceedings in mixed cases; and provided that the import of opium into China shall be subject to a customs duty of thirty taels per chest, plus an inland duty on the same, not to exceed eighty taels per chest, as li-ken for inland circulation. China has entered into Treaties with other States (*see Treaties of peace*).

Japan.

Area. Eng. sq. miles.	Population, 1882.
147,624	36,700,000

In 1854 a Convention was concluded by Sir James Sterling, on the part of Great Britain, at Nagasaki, for regulating the admission of British Ships into the Ports of Japan, and on August 26, 1858, a Treaty was
· concluded at Yeddo, between Great Britain and Japan, which provided for the appointment of Diplomatic and Consular Agents to reside at their respective capitals and ports. Japan has also entered into Treaty obligations with several other States.

Persia.

Area. Eng. sq. miles.	Estimated population.
307,000	7,000,000

A Treaty of Peace was concluded between Great Britain and Persia on March 4, 1857, by which the Shah undertook to withdraw from the territory and city of Herat and from every other part of Afghanistan, and to relinquish all claims and sovereignty on the same. The Agreement of August, 1851, for the suppression of the slave-trade in the Persian Gulf, was renewed. And another Convention was concluded, relative to Telegraphic communication between Europe and India, signed at Teheran November 20, 1865. The frontiers between Persia and Russia were settled by the Treaty of December 9, 1881.

Siam.

Area. Eng. sq. miles. 280,564	Estimated population. 5,750,000

A Treaty of friendship between Great Britain and Siam was signed at Bangkok on April 18, 1855, by which British subjects in Siam are to receive from the Siamese Government full protection and assistance to enable them to reside in Siam in all security, and to trade with every facility, free from oppression or injury on the part of the Siamese.

AFRICA.

Egypt.

Area. Eng. sq. miles. 10,687	Population, 1882. 6,817,000

Egypt is a Tributary State to Turkey. By a Firman addressed by the Sultan, dated February 13, 1841, Mehmet Ali Pasha, of Egypt, obtained the right of hereditary succession, of levying taxes in the

name of the Porte, coining of money, and raising a
number of troops for service in Egypt. A fourth of
the proceeds of the taxes was to go to the Porte. A
Firman, dated May 27, 1866, to Ismail Pasha, modified
the order of succession, and raised the amount of tribute
from 80,000 purses to 150,000 purses, or to £750,000
Turkish annually. A Firman of June 8, 1867, confirmed
the privilege of hereditary succession, and gave the right
to the Khedive of Egypt to conclude commercial and
other Treaties having no political significance. And
a Firman dated November 29, 1869, gave the right to
the Khedive to levy taxes in Egypt in the name of
the Sultan, and to contract foreign loans, the same
being submitted to the Sultan for approval. On June
8, 1873, all the privileges previously granted were
confirmed and collected in one Firman. By a Firman
dated August 14, 1879, Ismail Pasha ceased to be
Khedive, and Mehemed Tewfik, his son, was appointed
Khedive in his stead. By an Agreement signed at
Alexandria, July 31, 1875, the old system of consular
jurisdiction was abolished, and mixed courts were
established, where European and Native judges sit
together to try all mixed cases without respect to
nationality. The Suez Canal owes its origin to an
Act of Concession of the Viceroy of Egypt, dated
November 30, 1854, and January 5, 1856. A Con-
vention was entered into between the Viceroy of
Egypt and the Company of the Maritime Canal of
Suez, dated Cairo, January 30, 1866, which obtained

the sanction of the Sultan on March 19, 1866. A Convention was also signed on April 23, 1869, between the Khedive of Egypt and M. de Lesseps, for the construction of the same. In 1869 the British Government purchased from the Viceroy of Egypt 176,602 shares in the Canal for £4,000,000, by which Great Britain became part owners in the Suez Canal. The safety of the Canal having been threatened during the late insurrection in Egypt in 1882, the British Government, in a despatch dated January 3, 1883, to the British representatives at Paris, Berlin, Vienna, Rome, and St. Petersburg, expressed an opinion that an Agreement might be made to the following effect:—

1. That the Canal should be free for the passage of all ships in any circumstances.

2. That in time of war a limitation of time as to ships of war of a belligerent remaining in the Canal should be fixed, and no troops or munitions of war should be disembarked in the Canal.

3. That no hostilities should take place in the Canal or its approaches, or elsewhere in the territorial waters of Egypt, even in the event of Turkey being one of the belligerents.

4. That neither of the two immediately foregoing conditions shall apply to measures which may be necessary for the defence of Egypt.

5. That any Power whose vessels of war happen to do any damage to the Canal should be bound to bear the cost of its immediate repair.

6. That Egypt should take all measures within its power to enforce the conditions imposed on the transit of belligerent vessels through the Canal in time of war.

7. That no fortifications should be erected on the Canal or in its vicinity.

8. That nothing in the agreement shall be deemed to abridge or affect the territorial rights of the Government of Egypt further than is therein expressly provided.

Liberia.

Area. Eng. sq. miles.	Estimated population.
143,000	1,000,000

The Republic of Liberia was founded in 1822 by freed negroes from the United States of America and natives of Africa, who were organized by an American Society of Colonization, and since July 26, 1847, it declared itself independent.

Madagascar.

Area. Eng. sq. miles.	Estimated population.
2,300,000	3,500,000

An Island in the Indian Ocean on the coast of the African Continent. For a considerable time France asserted some possessory rights in the Interior of the Island, and these were recognized by certain tribes. By the Treaty of December 17, 1885, Madagascar assented that she should be represented abroad by the Government of the French Republic.

Morocco.

Area. Eng. sq. miles. 305,000	Estimated population. 614,000

A territory on the North-west corner of the African Continent, with the Mediterranean on the North and the Atlantic on the West.

A General Treaty between Great Britain and the Sultan of Morocco was concluded at Tangiers on December 9, 1856. By that Treaty each Power may appoint Consuls or other political Agents in the dominions of the other, with the usual guarantees for their security and privileges. British subjects in Morocco have perfect security for their person and property, and are free to exercise the rites of their own religion. No British subject is liable for the debts due from another person. In all criminal cases and complaints, and in all civil differences and disputes between British subjects the British Consul General is the sole judge and arbiter. In criminal and other cases between British and Moorish subjects, if the Plaintiff be British and the defendant a ·Moorish subject, the Governor of the town, or the Kadi, is the judge. If the plaintiff be a Moorish and the Defendant a British subject, the case is judged by the Consul General, with a right of appeal in either case to the the British Chargé d'Affaires or to the Moorish Commissioner for foreign affairs. All disputes between British subjects and the subjects or citizens of other foreign nations are decided by the Tribunals of the foreign Consuls without interference of the Moorish Government. The property of British subjects dying in Morocco belongs to the party named in the will, or, if there is no will, is taken charge of by the Consul General. In case of war, British subjects are to be allowed to depart to any part of the world they choose, and to carry with them their goods and property.

A Convention of Commerce and Navigation was concluded on December 9, 1856, between Great Britain and the Sultan of Morocco, which provided for reciprocal freedom of Commerce between the British dominions and the dominions of the Sultan of Morocco. The Sultan engaged to abolish all monopolies or prohibitions on imported goods, except tobacco pipes, opium, sulphur, saltpetre, arms and ammunition of war, and to abolish all monopolies of agricultural produce. A tariff of export duties was fixed.

A Convention was also concluded between Great Britain, Germany, Austria, Hungary, Belgium, Denmark, Spain, the United States, France, Italy, Morocco, the Netherlands, Portugal, and Sweden and Norway, dated July 3, 1880, for the settlement of the right of protection to interpreters and others by foreign representatives in Morocco.

South African Republic.

Approximate area. Eng. sq. miles.	Estimated population.
41,000	130,000

The boundaries of the South African Republic are defined in the Convention between Great Britain and

the Republic of February 27, 1884. The South
African Republic will conclude no Treaty or engagement with any State or nation other than the Orange
Free State, nor with any native tribe to the eastward
or westward of the Republic, until the same has been
approved by Her Majesty the Queen.

Tunis.

Approximate area. Eng. sq. miles. 44,726	Estimated population. 1,500,000

By a Treaty of May 28, 1881, entitled a Treaty of
friendship and *bon voisinage*, France was allowed to
occupy the territory militarily. France guaranteed
the execution of the existing Treaties between the
Regency and the different European Powers, and the
Diplomatic Agents of the French Republic abroad
were charged with the protection of Tunisian interests.
By another Treaty of November 3, 1883, the French
Government guaranteed a Tunisian loan and the con-
version of the Tunisian debt.

West Africa.

Area. Unknown.	Population. Unknown.

The Governments of Austria-Hungary, Belgium,
Denmark, France, Germany, Great Britain, Italy, the
Netherlands, Portugal, Russia, Spain, Sweden and
Norway, Turkey, and the United States having
agreed to concert together on the freedom of com-
merce in the basin of the Congo and its mouths,

Representatives of these Powers met at Berlin on November 15, 1884, under the Presidency of Prince Bismarck, who opened the Conference with these remarks:

"In convoking the Conference, the Imperial Government was guided by the conviction that all the Governments invited share the wish to bring the natives of Africa within the pale of civilization by opening up the interior of that Continent to commerce, by giving its inhabitants the means of instructing themselves, by encouraging missions and enterprises calculated to spread useful knowledge, and by preparing the way for the suppression of slavery, and especially the over-sea traffic in blacks, the gradual abolition of which was proclaimed by the Congress of Vienna of 1815, as the sacred duty of all the Powers."

The Conference commenced on November 15, 1884, and continued till February 26, 1885.

The General Act of the Berlin Conference is divided into seven Chapters.

Chapter I. is a Declaration relative to freedom of Trade in the Basin of the Congo, its mouths and circumjacent regions, declaring that the trade of all nations shall enjoy complete freedom, each Power only undertaking this engagement for itself; that all flags, without distinction of nationality, shall have free access to the whole coast line of the territory, rivers, and waters of the Congo and its affluents; that goods imported shall be subject to no other

taxes than such as may be levied for fair compensation for expenditure in the interest of trade ;
that merchandise imported shall remain free from
import and transit dues ; that no Power which exercises sovereign rights in the region shall be allowed
to grant therein a monopoly or favour of any kind in
matters of trade ; and that foreigners, without distinction, shall enjoy protection of their persons and
property, as well as the right of acquiring and trans-
ferring movable and immovable possessions.   Provisions are made relative to the protection of Natives, of
Christian Missionaries, Scientists, and Explorers, as
well as to freedom of commerce and religious tolera-
tion, including the free and public exercise of all
forms of Divine worship.   The Convention of the
Universal Postal Union was extended to the Conventional basin of the Congo.   And the International
Navigation Commission of the Congo was invested
with the right of surveillance on all parts of the
territory not under the Sovereignty of any Power.
Chapter II. is a declaration against using the territories
forming the Conventional basin of the Congo as a
market or means of transit for the trade in slaves.
Chapter III. is a declaration also relative to the
neutrality of the territories comprised in the Conventional basin of the Congo, providing that in case
of any serious disagreement originating on the subject
of or the limits of the territories, the Powers bind
themselves, before appealing to arms, to have recourse

to the mediation of one or more of the friendly
Powers. In a similar case the same Powers reserved
to themselves the option of having recourse to arbitration. Chapter IV. is an Act of navigation for the
Congo, declaring the navigation of the river, without
excepting any of its branches or outlets, free for the
merchant ships of all nations equally, the navigation
not to be subject to any restriction or obligation
not expressly stipulated in the Act. An International Commission was constituted, charged with
the execution of the Act, having power to decide on
necessary works, fixing dues, etc. Chapter V. is an
Act of Navigation for the Niger, declaring the navigation of the Niger, without excepting any of its
branches and outlets, to be free for the merchant
ships of all nations equally. Chapter VI. is a
declaration relative to the essential conditions to
be observed in order that new occupations on the
coasts of the African Continent may be held to be
effective. Any Power which henceforth takes possession of a tract of land on the coasts of the African
Continent outside of its present possessions, or which,
being hitherto without such possessions, shall acquire
them, as well as any Power which assumes a protectorate there, shall accompany the respective act
with a notification thereof, addressed to the other
signatory Powers of the present Act, in order to
enable them to make good any claims of their own.
And Chapter VII. contains general dispositions.

Zanzibar.

Approximate area. Eng. sq. miles.	Estimated population.
1186	200,000

The Sultanat of Zanzibar includes the Isles of Zanzibar, Pemba, and Mafia, on the East Coast of Africa. A Treaty of friendship, commerce, and navigation was concluded between Great Britain and the Sultan on April 30, 1886. By Art. XVI. subjects of her Britannic Majesty, as regards their person and property, enjoy within the dominions of the Sultan the rights of exterritoriality. The authorities of the Sultan have no right to interfere in disputes between subjects of Her Britannic Majesty among themselves, or between them and members of other Christian Nations. Such questions, whether of a civil or criminal nature, are to be decided by the competent Consular authorities.

AMERICA.

Argentine Confederation.

Area. Eng. sq. miles.	Estimated population.
1,094,200	2,942,000

The United Provinces of Rio de la Plata, the most important of which is Buenos Ayres, formed by their Confederation in May, 1853, revised in June, 1860, what is known as the Argentine Republic. Great Britain first concluded a Treaty with the Confederation on February 2, 1825.

Bolivia.

Area. Eng. sq. miles.	Estimated population.
47,000	2,203,000

The Republic of Bolivia exists since 1825. She once formed part of Peru, but the six provinces which now comprise her territory were united in Congress on August 6, 1825. The United States entered into a Treaty of Commerce with Bolivia November 13, 1837, and Great Britain on June 3 of the same year.

Brazil.

Area. Eng. sq. miles	Population, 1883.
3,218,000	12,333,375

Brazil was a Colony of Portugal from 1500. In 1821 she became independent, and in 1822 she was constituted into an Empire. By the mediation of Great Britain, Portugal made peace with Brazil in 1825. Brazil concluded Treaties of Commerce with France on January 8, 1826, with Austria on June 12, 1827, with Prussia July 9, 1827, and with Great Britain August 17, 1827.

Central America.

Area. Eng. sq. miles.	Estimated Population.
172,117	2,753,000

The Republic of Central America is a Confederation of four States, viz., Costa Rica, Guatemala, Honduras and San Salvador, and Nicaragua. The Act of federation was signed February 17, 1872.

Chile.

Area. Eng. sq. miles.	Population, 1864.
283,561	2,439,536

Chile declared her independence of Spain September 18, 1810. Originally she was part of the Empire of the Incas, within the Viceroyalty of Peru. Chile entered into a Treaty with the United States of America May 16, 1832. Her present constitution dates May 25, 1833.

Colombia.

Area. Eng. sq. miles.	Estimated population.
321,000	2,951,000

The present Republic of Colombia is the result of the dismemberment of the old Republic of the same name in 1831, which was divided into three Republics of New Grenada, Venezuela, and Equador. The United States entered into a Treaty with Colombia, on October 3, 1824, and Great Britain, on April 18, 1825.

Equador.

Area. Eng. sq. miles.	Estimated population.
250,000	1,005,000

Equador, which emerged from Colombia in 1830, constituted herself into an independent Republic in 1831. She is divided into three Departments, viz., Equador, Guayaquil, and Assuay.

Mexico.

Area. Eng. sq. miles. 751,423	Population, 1882. 10,448,000

Mexico declared her independence on September 6, 1810, but it was not till 1821–23 that the same was acknowledged by Spain. In 1822 Iturbide was elected Hereditary Constitutional Emperor, and in December Santa Anna proclaimed the Republic in Vera Cruz. In 1861 England, France, and Spain urged claims for losses incurred by their subjects resident in Mexico, and under a Convention the Allied Powers occupied Vera Cruz. In 1862 England and Spain withdrew from the occupation, their claims having been settled. But French troops remained, and an effort was made to reconstitute the Empire by the election to the Mexican Imperial Crown of the Austrian Archduke Ferdinand Maximilian. As soon, however, as the French troops withdrew, Maximilian was compelled to resign, and the Republic was restored.

Paraguay.

Area. Eng. sq. miles. 92,000	Population, 1879. 346,000

In 1811 the Creoles proclaimed a Republic, at the head of which they placed two Consuls. In 1814 Dr. Francia was elected dictator for life, with absolute power. On his death, in 1840, the Republic reverted to the form of government by two Consuls, but a President of the Republic has ever since been elected.

The present Constitution dates from November 25, 1870. The frontiers between Brazil and Paraguay were settled by the Treaty of January 9, 1872; between the Argentine Republic and Paraguay, by the Treaty of February 3, 1876. A Treaty of friendship, commerce, and navigation was concluded between Great Britain and the Republic of Paraguay on October 16, 1884.

Peru.

Area. Eng. sq. miles. 405,000	Population, 1876. 2,622,000

Peru gained her independence July 28, 1821. The United States entered into a Treaty with Peru on November 13, 1836, and Great Britain June 3, 1837. The present Constitution dates from 1858, modified November 10, 1866.

Uruguay.

Area. Eng. sq. miles. 68,551	Population, 1883. 65,550

The Republic of Uruguay is named from the river which separates her from the Argentine Republic, in Rio de la Plata. The State was constituted out of a portion of the Argentine Republic and of the ancient Banda Oriental. The present Constitution dates from September 10, 1829.

Venezuela.

Area. Eng. sq. miles. 633,000	Estimated population. 2,122,000

The Republic of Venezuela is one of the three independent States formed in 1831 on the dismemberment of the Republic of Colombia.

United States.

Area, with territories. Eng. sq. miles. 3,556,000	Population. 1881. 50,156,000

The United States of America declared themselves independent on July 4, 1776. By the Treaty of peace and friendship signed at Paris on September 3, 1783, Great Britain acknowledged the United States, viz. New Hampshire, Massachusetts Bay, Rhode Island, and Providence Plantations, Connecticut, New York, New Jersey, Pennsylvania, Delaware, Maryland, Virginia, North Carolina, South Carolina, and Georgia, to be free Sovereign and Independent States. The present Constitution dates from December 17, 1787. The United States now comprise thirty-eight States, besides some territories not yet recognized as States in union, and some Indian Territories. There are three distinct and independent powers in the United States, viz. the Executive in the President, the Legislative in Congress, and the Judicial in the Supreme Court.

Hawaii.

Area. Eng. sq. miles. 6541	Population, 1881. 80,000

The Hawaii are known under the name of the Sandwich Islands, and their independence was recognized by the United States on December 19, 1842, and by Great Britain on April 1, 1843.

Hayti.

Area. Eng. sq. miles. 9230	Estimated population. 800,000

The Island of San Domingo is the largest of the Antilles. The Treaty of Ryswick of 1697 ceded the half of the Island to the French, and the other half to Spain. The Blacks of the French portion revolted in 1791, and for a time the authority of the Metropolis was uncertain. In 1822 the whole Island was constituted a single Republic, under the name of Hayti, and she was recognized by France in 1825.

MATERIALS FOR A CODE

OF

INTERNATIONAL LAW.

CHAPTER I.

1. The State is a Community of persons, living within certain defined boundaries, subject to a constituted government, and freely united together for their common good.

"Civitas est cœtus perfectus liberorum hominum juris fruendi et communis utilitatis causa sociatus" (Grotius, "De Jure Belli et Pacis," Part I. c. 1, § xiv.). "Republica est cœtus multitudinis juris consensu et utilitatis communione sociatus" (Cicero, "De Rep.," I. c. 25). The State, not the rulers only, an abstract conception; the personification of a political Society is the subject matter of International Law.

2. The State, acting through its rulers, is a moral or juridical person, having rights and duties.

A moral person may be a group of persons or mass of property. The State, or a Corporation, or even a quasi-incorporate body, as a Joint Stock Company, is a moral person.

3. A State may consist of one or more people or nations.

"Nation" comes from *natus*, birth or origin, and means a multitude of people of the same race and language. The construction or reconstruction of States on the basis of nationality would be difficult, inasmuch as in most cases the population consists of mixed nationalities, the result of emigration, trade, and marriage. Nor would it be a certain benefit, for with the mingling of races there is increasing life and vigour.

4. A State includes all its colonies and dependencies.

5. A State must have a fixed locality. A nomadic population with no fixed territory does not constitute a State.

The Cherokee Nation v. *Georgia*, 5 Peter, U.S. Rep. 1; *Mackey* v. *Coxe*, 18 Howard, 100. The Cherokee nation was recognized as a people by Treaties made with them. See Kent's "American Law," vol. iii. p. 382.

6. The State may be one though its possessions are scattered.

Russia and the United States of America are compact States. But considerable portions of the British Empire are divided from one another by the Atlantic and Pacific Ocean.

7. A Corporation or private Association formed for the purpose of Trade, or for the advancement of any particular object, is not a State and has no international status.

The East India Company was represented by the British Government. The International Congo Association is under the sovereignty of the King of the Belgians. The Suez Canal Company is a Commercial Company.

8. A State is Sovereign as soon as it is regularly constituted and has sufficient power to defend itself.

9. The Sovereignty of a State consists in its right of independent action, without reference to the will of any other State.

" La Souveraineté confère à l'État qui en jouit une individualité politique, à régard des autres peoples, en vertu de la quelle il est considéré dans les relations internationales comme une persone morale ayant le droit de subsister par et pour soi même " (Ortolan, lib. i. c. 2, p. 12).

5

10. The provinces of a Sovereign State have no sovereignty of their own. They have no political personality, or right of separate correspondence with Sovereign States.

11. A State may, by express compact with any other State, consent to have its own sovereignty limited or qualified.

12. The Sovereignty of a State may be modified or limited by incorporation, real union, or federation with other States.

13. An incorporated union exists when both the internal and external sovereignty of each State is merged in the whole.

The United Kingdom of Great Britain and Ireland forms an incorporated union.

14. A federal Union exists when two or more States are under one Sovereign.

Sweden and Norway formed a federal Union under an hereditary Sovereign.

15. A federal Union also exists where any number of Sovereign States, while reserving for themselves their own autonomy for their internal matters, agree to unite together for certain

general interests, as defined by the Constitution.

A union which creates a new associated sovereignty will destroy the individual sovereignty of the uniting states. A union which creates no such new associated sovereignty will leave the sovereignty of each as it was. The United States of America constitute a federal Union under an elective President.

16. A State which acknowledges the suzerainty of another State is semi-sovereign.

17. A Tributary State may remain sovereign.

The simple payment of tribute would not of itself destroy the sovereignty of the State, but it is an evidence of weakness and diminished dignity which may mar its exercise.

18. A semi-protected State is independent in matters of internal administration, but subject as to its external relations.

19. A protected State, or one which has committed its own defence and its external relations into the hands of another State, is semi-sovereign.

Native States in British India are semi-sovereign States, under the protectorate of the United Kingdom. A fully protected State in India has a native dynasty

and native officials, but is under a British Resident,
who exercises a certain control in the internal administration of the State, as well as in its relations with
foreign Powers.

Indian nations on the Continent of America are
in the position of semi-sovereign States, under the
protectorate of the United States.

20. A State may lose its sovereignty by
its being annexed with, or ceded to, another
State, in which case the annexing or acquiring
State will become entitled to all the rights and
bound to all the obligations of the State annexed
or ceded.

21. The division of a State creates no forfeiture of previously recognized or vested rights
belonging to other States.

22. Treaty rights are not affected by any
revolution, nor are positive obligations of any
kind with other Powers, or with foreign creditors,
weakened by any such changes.

King of the Two Sicilies v. *Willcox*, 1 Simon's N. F.
301.

23. When any portion of territory is detached
from one State and united with another special
arrangements are made for apportioning its debts.

See the Convention between Austria, France, and Sardinia of September 9, 1860, relative to the liquidation of the Monte Lombardo-Veneto, N. R. T., vol. xvii. part 2, p. 29.

24. Internal sovereignty does not imply external sovereignty.

The first duty of a State after having acquired sovereignty and independence internally is to place itself in friendly relations with other members of the family of States.

25. The external sovereignty of a State is acquired by the express or implied recognition of its internal sovereignty on the part of other States.

Express recognition was given of the United Provinces by Spain in 1648; of the United States of America by the Treaty of Paris in 1783; of the Kingdom of Westphalia by Russia in 1807; of the French Republic by Great Britain in 1802; of the Confederation of the Rhine by Prussia in 1807; and of Napoleon as King of Italy by Austria in 1805. Also many Treaties with newly formed States directly involving recognition.

26. Each State is free to grant or refuse recognition to a newly formed State.

" Aucun état n'est tenu d'en reconnaître un nouveau,

tant qu'il y a encore lutte pour la formation du
nouvel état et que par conséquent il y a encore doute
sur l'existence de celui" (Bluntschli, § 31).

27. It is within the competence of a State to
refuse recognition to a newly formed State where
its independence is not yet secure and its power
of resistance remains doubtful.

28. Where a new State is formed of territories formerly belonging to another State, regard
should be had, in granting such recognition, to
existing duties towards the State from which the
revolutionized State seeks or has sought to
emerge, for so long as the struggle continues and
the issue is uncertain the recognition of the
revolutionized State may be said to favour one
party at the expense of the other.

See Lawrence's "Commentaire sur Wheaton" on
"De la conduite que les états étrangers peuvent
observer envers un état engagé dans une guerre civile."
The non-recognition of a State when sufficiently
established is inconvenient, since it deprives native
subjects residing in the same of the protection of the
Ambassador or other Minister in residence. A non-
recognized State has, moreover, no status in a Court of
justice. (See *The City of Berne* v. *the Bank of England*, 9 Ves. Jun. 347; *United States of America* v.

Wagner, 2 App. Cases, L. R. 582 ; *Yrisarri* v. *Clement*, 3 Bing. 432.)

29. In ordinary cases, on communication being made of the creation of a new State, or of the adoption by an old State of a new form of Government, or of the adoption of a new title by the Head of the State, recognition is granted as soon as such a State is in a condition to maintain international relations.

Where a State changes its institutions, say, from an Empire to a Republic, or *vice versâ*, or when the chief of the State assumes a new title, as from King to Emperor, or otherwise, a recognition of the fact when announced may be desirable and expected. A foreign sovereign State adopting the republican form of government, if recognized by the British Government, can sue in the British Courts in its own name so recognized (*United States of America* v. *Wagner*, 2 App. Cases, L. R. 582).

30. The recognition of a State does not imply an approbation of its constitution, or of its conduct in acquiring its independence.

CHAPTER II.

FRONTIERS OF THE STATE.

31. THE territory of a State includes whatever the State owns or has a right to possess.

32. A Colony is part of the State which establishes it.

33. The frontiers of a State are either natural or artificial.

34. Natural frontiers may be the sea, lakes, rivers, mountains, or unoccupied lands.

35. Artificial frontiers often consist of purely conventional lines made of stones, trenches, walls, trees, or other marks.

The delimitation of the frontiers between Afghanistan and Russia has given rise to much difficulty, in consequence of the inaccuracy of the maps available, and the desire on the part of Russia to reserve for herself the full military command of the junctions of the roads, while satisfying the English view by leaving the full command of the Zulfikar Pass to the Afghans. In September, 1885, commissioners were appointed to examine and trace upon the spot the details of the frontier. A Treaty has been concluded between Her Majesty and the Emperor of Russia, with the assent of the Ameer of Afghanistan, for the settlement of the frontier question.

36. The frontiers of a State are often traced on a map, and inserted in special Treaties determining the same.

37. A State may acquire territory by occupation, accession, transfer, cession, or conquest.

The right over a territory by simple discovery was once asserted by Spain and Portugal, but it is an insufficient title unless followed by occupation. Christian nations have asserted their rights over American territories, whilst reserving to the Indians their right of occupation of land possessed by them. The English Puritans who settled in New England purchased of the Indians the land which they intended to acquire. So did William Penn and the colony of Quakers in Pennsylvania. The right of occupation over their land has been conceded by Great Britain to the Maoris in New Zealand.

38. What belongs to no one (*res nullius*) may become territory of the State by discovery and first occupancy, provided the occupancy be

legitimate, that it be accompanied by a formal declaration, and that it be followed by effective possession.

39. A territory seized during war, and not restored at the conclusion of peace, becomes of right the property of the conqueror, and the title by conquest becomes in effect a title by cession.

40. A simple grant of territory, or a simple declaration of intention to possess it, or an occupation subsequently interrupted or abandoned, gives no right of property over the same.

41. The effective occupation of part of a territory, with the intention of total occupation, will involve the occupancy of the whole territory.

42. The right over a territory includes the right of using it as well as the right of adding to it. It includes the right of admitting any one to it and of excluding any one from it, the right of keeping it and the right of disposing of it.

43. Territorial sovereignty extends over both land and water within the territory, as well as over the natural increment of the land, as far as it can be defended from land, or as far as cannon-shot reaches.

44. Islands formed by alluvion belong to the lands which have contributed to their formation. When near the mainland, Islands are its natural dependencies; when at a sufficient distance, the right to an Island follows the same rules as in the case of any other territory.

The Anna, 5 Rob. Rep. 332.

45. The right of a State to its waters includes right to its seas, rivers, and canals.

46. A river flowing within the State is under the sovereignty of the same.

47. A river forming the frontier of several States is the common property of all, their respective frontiers being an ideal line in the midst of the river.

The right to the use of the whole river or bay for navigation is an easement or servitude common to both nations. *The Tame*, 3 Mason's U.S. 147.

48. The right of navigation in a river traversing several States is an imperfect right in many cases rendered perfect by special Treaties.

At the Congress of Vienna, it was decided that the navigation of rivers separating or traversing several

States shall be free from the point where they become navigable up to their mouth. The freedom of navigation of the Rhine was agreed to by the Congress of Vienna of 1815; of the Scheldt, Main, Meuse, Moselle, Neckar, by the Treaty of Westphalia of 1648; of the Elbe, by the Treaty of June 22, 1861; of the Po, by the Treaty of June 3, 1849, between Austria, Parma, and Modena; of the Vistula, by the Treaty between Prussia and Russia, 1815; of the Scheldt, by the Treaty between Belgium and Holland, 1839; of the Danube, by the Treaty of Bucharest of 1812, the Peace of Adrianople of 1829, the Treaty between Austria and Prussia of 1840, the Treaty of Paris of 1856, and the Public Act of 1865; of the Mississippi, by the Treaty between Great Britain and the United States of 1783; of the St. Lawrence, by the Treaty between England and the United States of 1854; of the Uruguay, by the Treaty between Brazil and the Oriental Republic of 1851; of the Paraguay, by the Treaty between Paraguay, France, and England of 1853, as well as by that between Brazil and the Argentine Republic of 1857; of the Amazon, by the Treaty between Brazil and Peru of 1851; of the Congo and Niger, by the International Treaty of 1885.

49. Where there is no Treaty for the free navigation of a river bordering on two States, the first who establishes a dominion over one of its banks would be held to have appropriated the

river also. Where there is difficulty in settling which State was the first, the dominion of each will extend to the middle of the river.

50. The right of navigating a river includes all the accessory rights of anchoring or fixing ships at the shore or islands which are within it, as well as of loading and discharging merchandise.

51. Territorial sovereignty extends over arms of the sea, such as bays, gulfs, and estuaries, provided they are enclosed; over ports, whether open, free, or closed; over mouths of rivers and adjacent parts of the sea enclosed by headlands.

Colchester v. *Brooke*, 7 Q. B. 339.

52. Territorial waters include such parts of the sea adjacent to the coast as are within one marine league of the coast measured from low-water mark.

53. Seas enclosed by lands are within the jurisdiction of the Countries within which they are situated.

54. A State may lose its territory or any part thereof by abandonment, by destruction, by transfer, or by conquest.

CHÁPTER III.

THE STATE AND ITS SUBJECTS.

55. THE State acts by its chief ruler **or by** such authorities as its constitution may determine. Whilst the attribute of sovereignty belongs to the State, the laws and customs of each Nation designate the power in the State in whom such sovereignty is to vest, and by whom it shall be exercised.

In the United Kingdom all sovereignty vests in the Queen, acting through her Ministers in Council, responsible to Parliament. In the United States of America the Executive Power is vested in the President, acting by and with the consent of the Senate. By the Constitution of the German Empire the Emperor represents the Empire internationally, declares war and concludes peace in the name of the Empire, enters into alliances with foreign Powers, as well as accredits and receives Ambassadors. And by the revised Federal Constitution, the supreme Executive authority of Switzerland is exercised by the Federal Assembly, one of whom is annually chosen President of the Confederation.

56. The Government of a State is its Executive power, to whom belongs the exercise of its effective sovereignty.

57. The subjects of a State are all persons born in the country, including the children of alien friends, persons born on board ships of the navy, or within the lines of the army, or in the house of its Ambassadors or Ministers abroad, and naturalized subjects or citizens. In a more general sense, the subjects of a State include foreign residents, whether domiciled or not.

58. International Law does not control the municipal Law of States, but takes cognizance of the same.

59. The definition of citizenship or alienage pertains to municipal Law.

60. The Laws regarding citizenship and the enjoyment of civil rights differ in many States.

In the United Kingdom every person born within the British Dominion is a British subject. Any person born out of her Majesty's Dominion of a father being

a British subject is a British subject, but any
British subject living abroad may cease to be such by
making a declaration of alienage. A British subject
naturalized in a foreign State is deemed to have ceased
to be a British subject, yet he may by making a declaration to that effect remain a British subject. A
married woman is deemed to be a subject of the State
of which her husband is for the time being a subject.
A widow, being a natural born British subject, who has
become an alien by or in consequence of her marriage
is deemed to be a statutory alien, and may at any time
during widowhood obtain a certificate of readmission
to British nationality. When the father, being a British
subject, or the mother, being a British subject, becomes
an alien, every child of either who during infancy has
become resident in the country where the father or
mother is naturalized, and has according to the laws of
such country become naturalized therein, is deemed to
be a subject of the State of which the father or mother
has become a subject, and not a British subject. When
the father, or mother, being a widow, has obtained a
certificate of readmission to British nationality, every
child of such father or mother is deemed to have
resumed the position of a British subject to all intents.
Where the father, or the mother, being a widow, has
obtained a certificate of naturalization in the United
Kingdom, every child of such father or mother who
during infancy has become resident with such father
or mother in any part of the United Kingdom is deemed

to be a naturalized British subject. A British subject becoming an alien is not thereby discharged from any liability in respect of any acts done before the date of his so becoming an alien. Where Her Majesty has entered into a Convention with any foreign State, to the effect that the subjects or citizens of that State who have been naturalized as British subjects may divest themselves of their status as such subjects, any person, being originally a subject or citizen of the State referred to, who has been naturalized as a British subject, may, within such limit of time as may be provided by the Convention, make a declaration of alienage; and from and after the date of his so making such declaration such person shall be regarded as an alien, and as a subject of the State to which he originally belonged (33 Vict. c. 14).

By a Convention between Her Majesty and the United States of America, signed at London May 12, 1870, Art. I., "British subjects who have become or shall become and are naturalized according to law within the United States of America as citizens thereof shall, subject to the provisions of Art. II., be held by Great Britain to be in all respects and for all purposes citizens of the United States, and shall be treated as such by Great Britain. And, reciprocally, citizens of the United States of America who have become or shall become and are naturalized according to law within the British dominion as British subjects shall, subject to the provisions of Art. II., be held by the United States to be in all respects and for all purposes British subjects, and shall be treated as such by the United States.

" Art. II.—Such British subjects who have become and are naturalized as citizens within the United States shall be at liberty to renounce their naturalization, and to resume their British nationality, provided that such renunciation be publicly declared within two years after the 12th day of May, 1870.

"Such citizens of the United States as aforesaid, who have become and are naturalized within the dominions of Her Britannic Majesty as British subjects, shall be at liberty to renounce their naturalization, and to resume their nationality as citizens of the United States, provided that such renunciation be publicly declared within two years after the exchange of the ratification of the present Convention.

" Art. III.—If any such British subject, naturalized in the United States, should renew his residence within the dominions of Her Britannic Majesty, Her Majesty's Government may, on his own application and on such conditions as that Government may think fit to impose, readmit him to the character and privileges of a British subject ; and the United States shall not in that case claim him as a citizen of the United States on account of his former naturalization.   In the same manner, if any such citizen of the United States as aforesaid, naturalized within the dominions of Her Britannic Majesty, should renew his residence in the United States, the United States Government may, on his own application, and on such conditions as that Government may think fit to impose, readmit him to the character and privileges of a citizen of the United States; and Great Britain shall not in that case claim him as a British subject on account of his former naturalization."

A supplementary Convention on the subject was concluded between Her Majesty and the United States February 27, 1871.

The principle of the French Law is that a child born of a French subject abroad is a French subject (Civil Code, § 10). And the same rule obtains in Italy, Germany, Spain, and other countries. But a State has a right to recognize as its subjects all born therein, as respects the obligation of military service; and therefore to exempt such subjects from such liability there is need of an accord between different countries (see § 175, p. 137).

61. The rights of aliens and the conditions for and rights consequent on naturalization are defined by Municipal Law.

In the United Kingdom real and personal property of every description may be taken, acquired, held and disposed of by an alien in the same manner in all respects as by a natural-born British subject; and a title to real and personal property of every description may be derived through, from, or in succession to an alien, in the same manner in all respects as through, from, or in succession to a natural-born British subject. An alien who has resided in the United Kingdom for a term of not less than five years, or has been in the service of the Crown for a term of not less than five years, and intends, when naturalized, either to reside in the United Kingdom or to serve under the Crown, may apply to one of Her Majesty's Principal Secretaries of State for a certificate of naturalization; and, if granted, the certificate will confer on such alien all political and other rights, powers, and privileges, and render him subject to all obligations which a natural-born British subject is entitled or subject to in the United Kingdom, with this qualification—that he shall not, when within the limits of the foreign State of which he was a subject previously to obtaining his certificate of naturalization, be deemed to be a British subject, unless he has ceased to be a subject of that State in pursuance of the laws thereof, or in pursuance of a Treaty to that effect (33 Vict. c. 14; 35 and 36 Vict. c. 39). In France, by the Civil Code, a foreigner enjoys the same civil rights as are conceded to a French citizen under the Treaty in force in the country to which the foreigners belong. But the Law of June 29, 1867, provides that a foreigner who, after having completed the twenty-fifth year of his age, has obtained the authority to establish his domicile in France, and has resided three years in the country, may be allowed to enjoy all the rights of French citizens, in virtue of a Decree of the Chief of the State on the report of the Minister of Justice. The delay of three years may be reduced to one when the party soliciting the naturalization has rendered signal service to the country, or has introduced an industry or useful invention, or has formed a great establishment of commerce or agriculture.

62. The practice of *escheatage*, under which foreigners were excluded from all right of inheritance in the State, either from a native born or an alien, and the *jus albinagii* or *droit d'aubaine*, by which all the property of a deceased foreigner, movable and immovable alike, was confiscated to the use of the State, to the exclusion of his heirs, are abolished by the Municipal Law of all liberal States and by special Treaties to that effect.

63. The subject, whether native-born or alien, owes to the State allegiance, obedience, and co-operation.

64. The State has no right to compel a foreign subject, not naturalized, to render civil or military service.

65. Nor has the State the right to punish a foreigner for an offence committed in a foreign land. (*See Extradition.*)

66. The State is not responsible to foreign States for the acts of, or the offences committed by, its subjects at home or abroad, provided it has taken every legal means for repressing and punishing such offenders, and has taken measures, as far as it is in its power, to prevent their recurrence.

CHAPTER IV.

67. THE State has a right to do whatever is calculated to secure its own preservation and independence.

68. The State has a right to acquire new countries or to enlarge its own possessions by discovery, colonization, or otherwise.

"Le prémier de tous les droits absolus ou permanents, celui qui soit de base fondamentale à la plus part des autres et au plus grand nombre des droits occasionels, est le droit de conservation de soi-même" (Ortolan, lib. i. c. 3, p. 55). "Un autre droit absolu ou permanent de tout état souverain, c'est d'être indépendant; c'est à dire de n'avoir à reconnaître, dans aucun de ces actes, l'autorité supérieure d'aucun autre état, isolé ou réuni à d'autres, de ne pas être tenu d'obéir aux injonctions impérative des autres puissances" (Ortolan, lib. i. c. 3, p. 56).

69. The State has a right to cede or alienate any portion of its territory within the limits of, and subject to, the safeguards imposed by its Constitution in that behalf.

70. Likewise the State may acquire or sell property by the same means and in the same manner as private individuals, that is, by purchase, cession, exchange, inheritance, or prescription.

71. The State has a right to increase its commerce, navigation, and fisheries; to work its mines and forests; to use freely its own lakes, rivers, and canals; to strike its own coinage, and to issue any kind of paper securities.

72. The right of trading with foreign countries is not a perfect right, nevertheless the refusal of a State to trade with any country is against comity.

73. The State has a right to augment its naval and military forces, or to construct fortifications within the limits necessary for purposes of defence, and has no right to oppose a similar exercise of right on the part of any other State.

When the excessive armaments of a State become

a source of danger to peace, a friendly State may demand an explanation and recommend disarmament.

See collective Note addressed by the Powers to Greece in order to induce the Hellenic Government to place their army on a peace footing (Correspondence respecting the affairs of Greece, June, 1886).

74. The State has a right to choose for itself whatever form of government it likes to adopt, and to change it at pleasure.

International Law only takes cognizance of the form of government in the State, in so far as it may affect the organs of international intercourse. In pure Monarchies, where the Sovereign has absolute power, his will alone has to be conciliated. In Constitutional or Republican States the will of the nation is an element of supreme influence.

75. The State has a right to exercise exclusive jurisdiction over all the inhabitants and property within the State, as well as over all suits and actions in courts of justice, whether civil or criminal, arising within its limits.

" C'est au Souverain à régler la forme et les solemnités des Contrats que ses sujets passent sur les terres de sa domination ; c'est à lui de prescrire les règles de procéder en justice. Le Souverain a aussi droit de faire des Loix qui assujettissent les Étrangers en plusieurs cas—

6

"1. Par rapport aux biens qu'ils en possèdent
    dans l'étendue de sa souveraineté;

"2. Par rapport aux formalités des contrats qu'ils
    passent sur ces territoires;

"3. Par rapport aux actes judiciaire qu'ils en plai-
    dent devant ses juges."

(Boullenois, "Traité de Loix," tom. i. p. 2.)

76. The laws of the State regulate the
manner and circumstances under which property
is held, bequeathed, and transferred.

77. Foreigners residing in any part of the
State are subject to its laws.

78. If a foreign subject commit a crime, he is
amenable to the criminal law of the country. If
two foreign subjects have a dispute among themselves it is to the local courts of justice they must
appeal.

But the submission of foreign residents to the
courts of the State presupposes confidence on their
part in the right administration of justice. Therefore where such confidence does not exist, foreign
subjects, by charters, privileges, concessions, or conventions, are made free from such jurisdiction, and made
subject to their own Consular jurisdiction. Such is
the case in the Levant, China, and Japan.

79. The State has a right to admit or to refuse admittance to any foreigner, and to establish regulations for the exercise of civil rights within its territory.

80. No State can by its laws affect persons or property out of its own country. Nevertheless the State has a right and also a duty to protect its subjects in foreign parts, and to see that the due and ordinary means of redress are open to them in the courts of justice, both civil and criminal.

81. Every State is bound to respect the rights of other States, and to fulfil its own obligations, whether moral or conventional, towards them.

82. The State must not allow plots or conspiracies to be organized within the State against the Sovereign of other States.

Conspirators against the Governments of, and public security in, other States should not be allowed to hatch their plans in a neighbouring and friendly State. The asylum granted to political exiles ought not to be abused. The publication of speeches and papers inciting to outrages amounting to murder and incendiarism should not be permitted, and any schemes for the destruction of life and property, by means of explosive manufactures or otherwise, ought to be prevented and frustrated by every means within the power of the Government.

By the criminal law of England all persons who conspire, confederate, and agree to murder any person, whether he be a subject of Her Majesty or not, and whether he be within the Queen's dominions or not, and whosoever shall solicit, encourage, persuade, or shall propose to any person to murder any other person, whether he be a subject of Her Majesty or not, and whether he be within the Queen's dominions or not, shall be guilty of a misdemeanor, and being convicted thereof, shall be liable, at the discretion of the Court, to be kept in penal servitude for any term not more than ten, and not less than five years, or to be imprisoned for any term not exceeding two years, with or without hard labour (24 and 25 Vict. c. 100, s. 4, amended by 27 and 28 Vict. c. 47, s. 2). *See Despatch from Her Majesty's Ambassador in Paris, March, 1858; Correspondence respecting the publication in the United States of incitements to outrages in England,* 1882.

83. A State is bound to uphold law and order, and to repress sedition, so as not to be a source of danger to itself and neighbouring States.

The first and second dismemberments of Poland

were justified by Russia, Prussia, and Austria, by the
fact that they were convinced by the experience of
the past of the absolute incapacity of the Republic
of Poland to give itself such a Government, or to live
peaceably under its laws in maintaining itself in a
state of independence.

84. A State is bound to provide for the
efficient and impartial administration of justice,
and to be punctual in the observance of Treaties
and in the payment of its debt, in capital, interest,
and sinking fund, according to the terms of its
obligations.

85. A State ought to exercise duties of be-
nevolence and humanity, and to do what is in
its power to promote the preservation and happiness of other States, especially in case of dis-
asters, such as famine, earthquake, distress, or
other calamities.

86. A State ought to carry on commerce with
other States, and should give no preference to
any State to the injury of another.

87. A State ought to receive Ambassadors or
other Diplomatic agents from any Sovereign
State with whom it intends to maintain relations
of friendship.

88. A permanently neutralized State is bound to avoid, in time of peace, taking any engagement which might prevent its observing the duties of neutrality in time of war, or any duties which are incompatible with the conditions of neutrality.

89. A permanently neutralized State may, however, enter into defensive alliances with other neutral States for the maintenance of their neutrality.

90. In other respects a permanently neutralized State is sovereign and independent, and may therefore lawfully exercise, in its intercourse with other States, all the rights and attributes of external sovereignty.

91. No hostility can be permitted within the territory of permanently neutralized States, nor the passage of an army or fleet through the limits of their territory. If a belligerent army or fleet forces its passage through its territory on land or sea, it is the duty of the permanently neutralized State to protest against the infringement of its rights.

CHAPTER V.

92. ALL Sovereign States, great or small, are equal in the eyes of International Law, such equality being subject to modification by compact or usage.

93. Republics take the same rank as monarchies and other Sovereign States.

In general Treaties the names of States are placed in alphabetical order, according to the French language. In political language States are known as of the first, second, or third rank, according to their power and political influence.

94. All Sovereign States are equal in matters concerning maritime ceremonials.

95. Salutes at sea between war vessels are not obligatory. They are regulated by the customary etiquette and courtesy.

CHAPTER VI.

THE SEA AND SHIPS.

96. THE sea is free to all. The ships of all nations are equally free to navigate every sea.

"Naturale jure omnium communia sunt illa; aer, aqua profluens, et mare" (Digest, lib. 1, cit. 8).

97. No territorial sovereignty exists or can be claimed beyond the three miles' zone.

"L'impossibilité de la propriété des mers résulte de la nature physique de cet élément qui ne peut être possédé et qui sert essentiellements aux communications des hommes et l'impossibilité de l'empire des mers résulte de l'égalité de droits et de l'indépendance réciproque des nations" (Ortolan, lib. ii. c. 7, p. 129).

98. Every nation has a right of fishing on the high sea.

The territorial waters of Her Majesty's dominions, in reference to the sea, mean such part of the sea adjacent to the coast of the United Kingdom, or of the coast of some other parts of Her Majesty's dominions, as is deemed by International Law to be within the territorial waters of Her Majesty, and for the purpose of any offence declared to be within the jurisdiction of the Admiral, any part of the open sea within one marine league of the coast measured from low-water mark being deemed to be open sea within the territorial waters of Her Majesty. An offence committed by a person, whether he is or is not a subject of Her Majesty, on the open sea, within the territorial waters of Her Majesty's dominions, is an offence within the jurisdiction of the Admiral, although it may have been committed on board or by means of a foreign ship (41 and 42 Vict. c. 73). *Reg.* v. *Klein,* 2 Ex. Div., L.R. 63; *Reg.* v. *Lopez; Rex* v. *Sattler,* Dears and B.C. 525; *Rex* v. *Jones,* 2 C. and K. 165.

99. International Law recognizes only two classes of ships, viz. vessels of war and merchant vessels.

100. A war vessel is an armed ship employed in the public military service of the State. A war vessel is part of the national territory. On board such ship no other sovereignty is recognized, but that of the Government to which the ship belongs.

101. A ship of war entering within the maritime territory of a friendly State is entitled to the

same privileges which are extended to the person
of the Sovereign.

102. A ship of war is not subject to local
jurisdiction in a foreign port.

Proceedings against ships of war cannot be instituted (*The Schooner "Exchange"* v. *McFadden*, 7
Cranch, 135). No maritime lien can be enforced
against them (*The "Prinz Fred,"* 2 Dod. Adm. 451 ;
"The Constitution," 4 P. D. 39).

"Le droit d'éxtérritoralité est plein et entier pour
les navires de guerre. Dans les ports qui leur ont été
ouverts ils sont généralement exempts de la visite des
douanes quoique à vrai dire cette visite ne constitue pas
un act de jurisdiction" (*Ortolan's "* Règles," liv. ii. c. 10).

103. The proofs of the public character of a
ship of war are the flag, the public commission,
and the public officers in command. The commission would be of itself sufficient, if duly
authenticated, but the visible signs are the flag
and pennant.

104. A merchant ship on the high sea is
subject to the Municipal Law of the country to
which the ship belongs. A crime committed on
board a merchant ship by any of the officers or
crew comes within the jurisdiction of the tribunals of that country.

105. But when a merchant ship enters the harbour of a friendly State, she owes allegiance to that State and is subject to the laws of the same.

106. A steamer owned by private individuals and carrying mails for the Post-Office, on contract, and having on board a servant of the Post-Office, is a merchant vessel or a common carrier for hire. Where, however, the vessel belongs to the Sovereign, her immunity as a public ship would not be lost by her being used partially for trading purposes.

The "Parlement Belge," 42 L. T. 273. (See Convention with France respecting immunities of Mail Ships.)

107. The nationality of a ship is determined by the nationality of her owners or otherwise, according to the maritime law of the State to which she belongs.

The national character of the ship must be declared before a clearance can be obtained at the Customs (17 and 18 Vict. c. 102, s. 102).

108. The ship's papers are those required by the Municipal Laws of the State to which she belongs. They usually are the Certificate of Registry, the Charter-party, the Bills of Lading, and the Bill of Health.

109. Pirate ships have no national character and no recognized position. No nation ought to receive a pirate ship into its territory. Piracy is a criminal act, and a ship employed in piracy may be captured.

The " Le Louis " v. *Dodson*, Adm. Rep. 232.

110. Property found in and taken from a pirate ship ought to be restored to the innocent owner.

Questions of piracy are under the jurisdiction of the Court of Admiralty. Ships taken from pirates are liable to condemnation as droits and perquisites of Her Majesty in her Office of Admiralty (13 and 14 Vict. c. 26 ; 20 and 21 Vict. c. 3). When restored to the innocent owner he ought to pay a sum of money equal to one-eighth part of their value, to be distributed among the captors.

111. The slave-trade is declared to be piracy by English Law, and by Treaty most civilized States have agreed to treat slave ships as pirates.

If any British subject, wherever residing, and whether within the dominion of Great Britain or of any foreign Country, or in the Colonies, shall, within the jurisdiction of the Admiralty, knowingly convey or assist in conveying persons as slaves, or to be dealt with as slaves, or ship them for that purpose, he will be deemed guilty of piracy, felony, and robbery (5 Geo. 4 c. 113, and 36 & 37 Vict. c. 88).

CHAPTER VII.

SECTION I.—AMBASSADORS AND DIPLOMATIC AGENTS.

112. EVERY Sovereign State has a right to send and to receive public Ministers to and from any State with whom it may desire to live in peace and friendship.

113. A semi-sovereign State has no right to send or to receive public Ministers; nor a province of a State, or a dependent or suzerain State, or a federal State, or an unrecognized State; nor a deposed Sovereign, or one who has abdicated.

Princes and States have business with one another, and, not being able to communicate in person without compromising their dignity or the business itself, they use the instrumentality of some Ministers to whom they give a public character.

114. Diplomatic Agents differ in character and position, according as their mission is one for special negotiation, etiquette, and ceremonial, extraordinary or ordinary.

115. Diplomatic Agents are of four classes, viz. Ambassadors, Envoys or Ministers, Chargés d'Affaires accredited to the Sovereign, and Chargés d'Affaires accredited to the Foreign Minister.

There is great advantage in appointing a man of position and dignity as Ambassador to a foreign Court. Men of letters have often filled such functions with high credit. The Ambassador ought to be a man of learning and erudition, but still more a man of ripe wisdom, a man of experience, and of high moral qualities.

116. Diplomatic intercourse within the cognizance of International Law is limited to what pertains to the civil interests of States. The Ambassador or public Minister ought therefore to be a civilian, and not an ecclesiastic.

The Pope now is a spiritual, not a civil power. So long as he was the Sovereign of a State, however small, he was a civil ruler, competent to send or receive an Ambassador. When he ceased to be a civil ruler, the reason for his maintaining official diplomatic

intercourse with States ceased to exist.   The question
of establishing diplomatic intercourse between the
United Kingdom and the Pope has frequently been
brought before the British Parliament, but constitutional difficulties oppose it.   The Bill of Rights
(1689) and the Act for settling the succession to the
Crown provided that all and every person or persons
who was, were, or should be reconciled, or should
hold communion with the See of Rome, should be
excluded, and for ever become incapable to inherit,
possess, or enjoy the Crown.   A Legate or Nuncio
sent by the Pope, having functions purely spiritual,
would not enjoy the protection of the Law of Nations,
but simply the security of public faith in the place
where he resides.   The Diplomatic Corps accredited
to the Holy See consists of Ministers from Austria-
Hungary, Bavaria, Belgium, Bolivia, Brazil, Chile,
France, Monaco, Nicaragua, Peru, and Portugal.

117. The State that appoints a mission has
a right to choose a proper person for the same ;
nevertheless, care should be taken to nominate
a person who shall be agreeable—a *persona grata*
—to the State to which he is sent.

A *persona grata* is one of courteous manner and
respectful demeanour ; one who has on no previous
occasion given offence to the State to which he is to
be accredited.   The American Government once ap-

pointed a French subject, but naturalized in the United States, as Ambassador to France, and the question arose as to whether a person naturalized in a foreign State, on returning to his native country, is understood to reacquire his native domicile; whether such naturalized foreign subject could, on his return to his native land, claim the immunities of a foreign Ambassador; and whether, if he were so appointed, he could protect the interest of the Sovereign he represented while yet being faithful to his native Country.

118. A Diplomatic Agent should receive clear and explicit instructions, expressing the intentions of the Sovereign or of the State which he is to represent.

He is also supplied with Letters of Credentials, showing the character he bears. These he must communicate to the Sovereign to whom he is sent, by the instrumentality of the Master of the Ceremonies, or of the Secretary of State for Foreign Affairs.

119. On his arriving at his post, a Diplomatic Agent notifies his arrival to the Minister for Foreign Affairs, and his reception by that Minister is an evidence of recognition of the Government or of the State which he comes to represent.

120. Where a public audience is given by the

Sovereign to any foreign Minister specially accredited to the State, the usual formalities and etiquette are to be used.

Questions of etiquette and ceremonials have no longer the force which they had in former days. Nevertheless, an Ambassador who represents a Sovereign State must remember that any honour and respect he may receive, or any indignities which may be imposed upon him, are paid to or imposed on the State which he represents. In the relations of European States with China, the unwillingness of the Emperor to admit foreign Ambassadors to his presence, and his offers to do so on conditions of a servile character, had not a small influence in bringing about public hostilities. At the end of the war, the unseemly dictation was withdrawn, and etiquette regulations were settled for an audience to be given to the Representatives of foreign Powers by the Emperor of China at Peking on July 7, 1873.

121. Foreign Ministers, duly accredited by their Sovereigns, rank among themselves, in the State where they reside, in order of precedence according to the notification of their arrival, each, however, in the class to which he belongs.

In Catholic countries the Nuncio of the Pope is allowed to stand first in rank. Not so in Protestant States.

122. The oldest Minister at the Court in the order of such notifications is the Dean of the Diplomatic Corps.

123. An Ambassador enters into his appointment by the production of his letters of credentials, and retires from it by the presentation of his letters of recall.

124. An Ambassador is the public agent of the State which he represents. He is the mandatory and representative of his Sovereign.

125. A Diplomatic Agent, like any other agent, must act in conformity with his instructions, and must not commit the State which he represents by any act of his own for which he is not fully authorized.

126. It is the duty of a Diplomatic Agent to watch over the interests of the State which he represents, and to report to the Minister of Foreign Affairs every circumstance which he may deem of importance or useful to report, especially every movement of troops or other indications of policy which may affect his own or other States.

"Gli Ambasciatori," said Guicciardini, "sono l'occhio

e l'orecchio degli Stati" (Ambassadors are the eye and the ear of States).

127. In his relations with the Sovereign or public officers of the State in which he resides, it is the duty of the Diplomatic Agent to exercise the utmost care and discretion, to use urbane and conciliatory language, and to maintain in all his dealings a due regard to justice, as well as a calm and moderate spirit.

SECTION II.—RIGHTS OF DIPLOMATIC AGENTS.

128. An Ambassador has a right of access to, or of personal audience from, the Sovereign to whom he is accredited.

129. He has the right to maintain religious worship at the Embassy for himself, his household, the members of the Legation, and other friends, the same being his own country men or women.

130. The person of an Ambassador is sacred. He is free from arrest, and is not amenable to the pursuit of a court of justice.

131. The house of a Diplomatic Agent is sacred and extra-territorial.

132. But he has no right to use his house as an asylum, or for the purpose of protecting other persons who do not belong to him from criminal pursuit.

133. The Ambassador is not liable to taxes, and is exempt from the payment of rates on the house he occupies.

134. The immunities of a Diplomatic officer extend to every member of his own household.

135. A Diplomatic officer cannot sue or be sued in his own name.

136. The powers of an Ambassador are always revocable.

137. The functions of an Ambassador terminate with the extinction of the Sovereignty of the State where he resides, with the death or abdication of the Sovereign of either that State, or of the State which he represents, with the withdrawal of his powers, with the rupture of relations between the States, or with the accomplishment of the mission, when the same was of a temporary character.

SECTION III.—CONSULS.

138. A Consul is an officer—either purely commercial or semi-public and commercial—appointed by a Sovereign to reside abroad for the purpose of protecting the commercial interests of merchants of his own nationality in the place where he resides.

The word "Consul" has been used for a political as well as a commercial office. In Rome, after the expulsion of the Tarquins and the abolition of Royalty, the Romans substituted, for one sole King, two Magistrates elected annually by the people, to whom they gave the title of Consuls. But again the consular authority was united with the kingly. In France the law of 19 Brumaire, An. VIII., established a provisional Government of three Members, called Consuls, and soon after the First Consul was charged with supreme authority.

The Consul is a public or semi-diplomatic agent, inasmuch as he represents the State by whom he is sent, and cannot exercise his functions until he has been accepted by the Sovereign to whose State he has been sent.

139. A Consul has no right to interfere in political matters, except in cases where there is no political officer to whom he can appeal in cases of difficulty.

140. The Consular duties are exercised by Consuls-General, Consuls, and Vice-Consuls.

141. As soon as the Consul arrives in the place to which he is appointed, he must exhibit his commission to the authorities of the country, in order that he may obtain their sanction to his appointment, called an Exequatur, which secures to him the enjoyment of such privileges, immunities, and exemptions as have been enjoyed by his predecessors, or as are usually granted to Consuls in the country where he is to reside.

142. Unlike the Ambassador, the Consul is subject to the laws of the country in which he resides.

143. The residence of the Consul is not extra-territorial, and he is bound to pay rates and taxes.

144. The duties of the Consul are—

(*a*) To watch over the commercial interests of the subjects of the country he represents, and to assist them with his advice in all doubtful emergencies.

(*b*) To see that the commercial treaties in force are duly observed.

(*c*) To attend to any grievances and difficulties in which seamen of his country may be involved.

(d) To relieve any distressed seaman belonging to his country; to allow him a sum, and give a free pass to such as may wish to return home.

(e) To claim and recover all wrecks, cables, and anchors belonging to his country-men, and to pay the usual salvage.

(f) To receive any protest at the hand of any masters of vessels.

(g) To administer an oath as a magistrate, and do notarial acts.

145. It is the duty of the Consul to send an annual or quarterly statement of the trade of the place where he resides to the Government he represents.

146. Where specially authorized by the State which he represents, or by special privilege, capitulation, or treaty to that effect, the Consul exercises a criminal and civil jurisdiction over the subjects of his own country.

147. Under the 12 & 13 Vict. c. 68 (1849), and the Consular Marriage Act, 1868, a British Consul may celebrate a marriage between persons who have resided one month in the district, both, or one of them, being a British subject.

CHAPTER VIII.

TREATIES.

148. A TREATY is a contract between States.

Treaties between European States used to be headed, " In the name of the very holy and indivisible Trinity." The Treaty of Berlin of 1878 was headed, " In the name of Almighty God; " the Treaty with Zanzibar was headed, " In the name of the most high God." Treaties are ended with, " In witness whereof the respective Plenipotentiaries have signed it, and have affixed to it the seal of their arms."

149. A Treaty which affects the interests of the State is a public Treaty. A Treaty which refers to the person or family of the Sovereign only is a private Treaty.

150. When a Sovereign contracts " for himself and his successors," it is a real Treaty, and the rights and obligations accruing from it pass to the State and its subsequent rulers.

151. A public Treaty attaches to the body of the State and subsists as long as the State exists, unless the period of its duration is expressly limited. A personal Treaty expires with the death of the Sovereign who contracted it.

152. Every Sovereign State has a right to contract public Treaties with foreign States, the constitutional or fundamental laws of the State determining with whom rests the authority of negotiating the same and the conditions for their sanction and authority.

153. A Semi-sovereign State has no right to enter into a public Treaty.

154. When a Treaty is to be concluded by a Minister Plenipotentiary under instructions from his Sovereign or the State, his powers to that effect must be shown to the contracting parties and be recognized by them as in due form.

155. A Treaty negotiated by a Minister Plenipotentiary must be ratified by the Sovereign or State, and is not in force until such Ratification has been notified.

7

156. The requisites for the validity of a Treaty are—(1) the capacity of the parties to the contract ; (2) the consent of the contracting parties freely given, under no mistake, fraud, or violence.

157. Treaties are written in the language of each contracting party.

Up to the middle of the eighteenth century Treaties were written in Latin as a common language. Afterwards the French language began to be used as the language of diplomacy. In later time, however, the custom has been introduced for each nation to use its own language, both in diplomatic correspondence and in the preparation of Treaties. The Treaty of Vienna of 1815 contained the following clause : " The French language having been exclusively used in all the copies of the present Treaty, the Powers which have been parties to the same recognize that the use of this language will not carry consequences for the future ; each Power reserving to itself the right, in future negotiations and conventions, to adopt the language which it has hitherto used in its diplomatic relations, without danger that the present Treaty may be cited as an example contrary to established usages." The recent Treaties between Great Britain and Austria-Hungary were written in three languages, viz. English, German, and Magyar.

158. A Treaty is binding on the contracting parties only.

159. A public Treaty is inviolable. The principle, "Sanctitas pactorum gentium publicorum," is a law binding on all States.

160. A Treaty is obligatory, whatever be the difference of religion among the contracting parties.

161. No Power can liberate itself from the engagements of a Treaty, or modify the stipulations thereof, unless with the consent of all the other contracting Powers, by means of an amicable arrangement.

162. A Treaty entered into by several States for their mutual protection, or for the guarantee of another State, involves a joint obligation to use such means as may be required to accomplish the object.

A contract by two or more persons may be joint only or joint and several. If joint only, it is the obligation of all the parties together, and of none separately; if joint and several, it is obligatory on each party separately and on all unitedly. If a covenant to do a particular act be entered into with

several persons generally, they have all a *primâ facie*
or joint interest in the performance of it. But what
is *primâ facie* only a joint obligation may be construed to be several, if the interest of each of the
parties appear upon the face of the deed to require
that construction. In an obligation *in solidum* each
contractor engages to do the same thing, but such
obligation is not presumed. It must be express.

A guarantee is a contract by one person to be
answerable for the payment of some debt, or the performance of some act or duty, in case of the failure of
another person, who is himself primarily responsible
for the payment of such debt or the performance of
the act agreed to be done. The obligation of the
guarantor is not direct, but subsidiary or accessory
to that of the principal debtor. The guarantor agrees
to satisfy the obligation of the debtor, if the debtor
does not do it himself, and it is the duty of the
creditor first to use his endeavour to get the payment
from the debtor. And the same rule would obtain in
the case of a guarantee to protect a State, with this
difference—that whereas in the guarantee of a debt
the creditor has the power to enforce the guarantee,
in the guarantee to protect a State the State itself
so guaranteed has not the power to enforce the contract. Vattel said, "As no nation is obliged to do
anything for another nation which that other is
capable for herself, it follows that the guarantor is
not bound to give his assistance except when the

party whose State *he* has guaranteed is unable by herself to obtain justice."

163. A Treaty may be for a period of time or indefinite as to its duration.

164. A Treaty dates from the day when it was signed, and not from the date of its ratification.

165. When the period of its duration is fixed and the condition of the parties has not been altered, no one has a right to withdraw from it unless permitted by the other party or parties.

166. When the Treaty is to continue in force indefinitely unless notice be given, the obligation will continue unimpaired till such notice be given and accepted.

167. Treaties stipulating for permanent rights and general arrangements do not cease to be in force on the occurrence of war, but are only suspended whilst the war lasts, and, unless waived by the parties, revive on the return of peace.

168. A Treaty is construed according to the plain and obvious meaning of the language employed, technical words being construed ac-

cording to their technical meaning, the intentions of the parties being discovered by reference to the language of the whole instrument.

169. Treaties affecting public rights are binding as such only on the States between whom the Treaties in question were concluded; nevertheless, in so far as they express rights and obligations of a moral character, or establish relations of general convenience, they have a wider authority and more general application, and may be said to constitute part of the conventional law of civilized States.

170. The mutual rights and duties of States incident to a state of peace, friendship, and good understanding are either secured by the constitution or by the fundamental laws of the respective countries, or are expressly provided for by Treaties.

171. The ratification of a Treaty consists of a writing signed by the Sovereign or chief of the State and sealed with his seal, whereby he approves of the contents of the Treaty concluded in his name, and promises to execute the same faithfully and in all points.

172. The Ministers of the contracting parties exchange these ratifications within the time agreed upon, and it is only after the exchange of the same that a Treaty becomes obligatory.

In the United Kingdom Treaties are not laid before Parliament until they have been ratified. It is usual, however, in case of a Treaty affecting interests of importance, as in the case of a Treaty of commerce, or a Treaty involving financial operations which are specially within the cognizance of the House of Commons, to give such time for the exchange of ratification as will allow of Parliament being consulted on the subject. In cases where a considerable time must elapse in consequence of great distances for the ratification, counterpart copies of the Treaty, signed and sealed by the Plenipotentiaries on behalf of their respective Sovereigns, are mutually delivered, and all its provisions and arrangements are forthwith put into execution, subject in all cases to the ultimate ratification of the Treaty. The Agreement between the Government of Great Britain and China for the settlement of the Yünnan case, official intercourse, and trade between the two countries was signed at Chefoo, September 13, 1876, and with an additional article regulating the traffic in opium, signed in London July 18, 1885, was ratified on May 6, 1886.

CHAPTER IX.

173. THE subjects of the contracting parties have the right to enter, travel, and reside in any part of the territory of the other, and there to enjoy full security and protection for themselves and their families in their persons and property, whether real or personal.

174. They have the right to hire and occupy houses and warehouses, manufactures, shops, and premises, for purposes of their commerce.

175. They have the right to acquire and dispose of, whether by purchase, sale, donation, exchange, marriage, testament, succession *ab intestato*, or in any other manner whatever, every description of property which the laws of the country may permit any foreigner, of whatever nation, to hold.

176. The heirs and representatives of the contracting parties have the right to succeed to, and take possession of, such property, either in person, or by agents acting on their behalf, in the ordinary form of law, in the same manner as the subjects of the country; and in the absence of such heirs and representatives the property is treated in the same manner as the like property belonging to the subjects of the country under similar circumstances.

177. In the event of any subjects dying without will or testament in the dominions of the other contracting party, or in the absence of lawful heirs or representatives, the Consul-General, Consul, and Acting Consul of the nation to which the deceased may belong, in so far as the laws of the country will permit, and after a duly made and attested inventory has been signed by him, takes possession and charge of the property which the deceased may have left for the benefit of his lawful heirs and creditors, giving immediate notice of the death to the authorities of the country.

178. The subjects of each State in the dominions of the other have the right of exemption

from all compulsory military service whatever, whether in the army, navy, or national Guard or Militia, and of exemption also from all judicial and municipal functions whatever, as well as from all contributions, whether pecuniary or in kind, imposed as a compensation for personal service, and also from forced loans and military exactions or requisitions.

179. They have the right to enjoy the most perfect and entire liberty of conscience, without being molested or disturbed on account of their religious belief, or to be molested or disturbed in the proper exercise of their religion in private houses, or in the churches, chapels, or places destined for worship, provided that in so doing they observe the decorum due to Divine worship, and the respect due to the laws of the country.

180. They have the right to bury the subjects of either State, who may die in the territory of the other, in convenient and adequate places to be appointed and established by the resident subjects for that purpose, with the knowledge of the local authorities, or in such other place of sepulture as may be chosen by the friends of the deceased; the funeral or sepulchres of the dead

not being disturbed in any wise or upon any account.

181. They have the right of resort to the courts of justice for their judicial recourse, on the same terms which are usual and customary with native subjects, for which purpose they may either appear in proper person, or employ in the prosecution or defence of their rights such advocates, solicitors, notaries, agents, and factors, as they may judge proper in all their trials at law. They have also free opportunity to be present at the decision or sentence of the tribunals in all cases which may concern them, and enjoy in such cases all the rights and privileges accorded to native subjects.

182. If at any time any interruption of friendly intercourse, or any rupture, should take place between the contracting States, the subjects or citizens of either of the two contracting parties who may be within any of the territories, dominions, or settlements of the other, if residing upon the coasts, are allowed *six months*, and if residing in the interior *a whole year*, to wind up their accounts and dispose of their property, and

a safe-conduct is given to them to embark at the port which they themselves shall select; and even in the event of a rupture, all such subjects or citizens of either of the two contracting parties who are established in any of the territories, dominions, and settlements of the other, in the exercise of any trade or special employment, have the privilege of remaining and of continuing such trade and employment therein, without any manner of interruption, in full enjoyment of their liberty and property as long as they behave peaceably, and commit no offence against the laws; and their goods and effects, of whatever description they may be, whether in their own custody or entrusted to individuals or to the State, are not liable to seizure or sequestration, nor to any other charges or demands than those which may be made upon the legal effects or property belonging to native subjects or citizens of the country in which such subjects or citizens may reside. In the same case, debts between individuals, property in public funds, and shares of companies are never confiscated, sequestered, or detained.

See British Treaties with Uruguay, August 26, 1842; *Guatemala, February* 20, 1849; *Siam, April*

18, 1855; *Swiss Confederation, September* 6, 1855; *Honduras, August* 27, 1856; *Nicaragua, February* 11, 1860; *Salvador, April* 16, 1863; *United States of Colombia, February* 16, 1866.

Treaties of peace and friendship have been concluded between the following States:—

See also Treaties of Commerce and Navigation.

EUROPEAN STATES.
Austria and Austria-Hungary.

Prussia and Russia, November 8, 1846; United States, May 8, 1848; Sardinia, August 6, 1849; Russia, etc., March 30, 1856; Moldo-Wallachia, February 19, 1858; France, November 10, 1859; Italy, October 3, 1866; Siam, May 17, 1869; China, September 2, 1869; Japan, October 18, 1869; Hawaii, June 18, 1875.

Bavaria.

Russia, August 22, 1866.

Belgium.

Persia, July 14, 1841; Nicaragua, March 27, 1849; Guatemala, March 27, 1849; Peru, May 16, 1850; Italy, April 9, 1863; Orange Free States, April 1, 1874; Transvaal, December 11, 1875; Morocco, July 3, 1880.

Denmark.

Prussia, July 2, 1850; Russia, May 25, 1851; Persia, November 30, 1857; Great Britain, etc., June 10, 1863; Switzerland, February 13, 1875; Morocco, July 3, 1880.

France.

Two Sicilies, May 12, 1847; Guatemala, March 8, 1848; Chile, October 7, 1849; Honduras, February 22, 1856; Turkey, etc., March 30, 1856, August 19, 1858; Siam, August 15, 1856; Sandwich Islands, October 29, 1857; Salvador, January 2, 1858; China, June 27, 1858; Japan, October 9, 1858; Nicaragua, April

11, 1859; Sardinia, November 10, 1859; Annam, June 5, 1862, March 15, 1874; Madagascar, September 12, 1862, August 8, 1868; China, October 25, 1860; Servia, January 18, 1863; Germany, May 10, 1871; Burmah, January 24, 1873; Uruguay, August 18, 1873; Morocco, July 3, 1880.

Germany.

(North Germany previous to 1870; Germany from 1870.)

Denmark, July 2, 1850; Argentine Confederation, September 15, 1857; Turkey, etc., August 19, 1858; Paraguay, August 1, 1860; Chile, February 1, 1862; Liberia, October 31, 1867; Japan, February 20, 1869; Mexico, August 28, 1869; Salvador, January 13, 1870; France, May 10, 1871; Costa Rica, May 18, 1875; Tonga, November 1, 1875; Samoa, January 24, 1879; Hawaii, March 25, 1879; Morocco, July 3, 1880; Mexico, December 5, 1882; Madagascar, May 15, 1883; Corea, November 26, 1883· Republic of South Africa, January 22, 1885.

Prussia. ·

Austria, November 8, 1847; Denmark, May 23, 1851 (see Germany).

Great Britain.

Borneo, May 27, 1847; Liberia, November 21, 1848; Argentine Confederation, November 24, 1849; Costa Rica, November 27, 1849; Dominica, March 6, 1850; Peru, April 10, 1850; Equador, May 3, 1851; Hawaii, July 10, 1851; Afghanistan, July 13, 1855, May 26, 1879; Siam, April 18, 1855; Turkey, etc., March 30, 1856, August 19, 1858; Honduras, August 27, 1856; Persia, March 4, 1857; Japan, August 26, 1858; Nicaragua, February 11, 1860; Greece, etc., June 10, 1863; Madagascar, January 27, 1865; Ashanti, February 15, 1874; Portugal, December 11, 1875; Samoa, August 28, 1879; Tonga, November 29, 1879; Servia, February 7, 1880; Equator, October 18, 1880; Morocco, July 3, 1880; Montenegro, January 22, 1882; Corea, November 26, 1883; Spain, December 1, 1883; Transvaal, February 27, 1884; Paraguay, October 16, 1884; Zanzibar, April 30, 1886.

Greece.

Great Britain, June 10, 1863.

Italy.

Turkey, August 19, 1858; Belgium, April 9, 18Γ3; Austria, October 3, 1866; Burmah, March 3, 1871; December 26, 1872; Morocco, July 3, 1880.

Sardinia.

New Grenada, August 18, 1847; Austria, August 6, 1849; France, November 10, 1859, February 11, 1860.

Two Sicilies.

France, May 12, 1847.

Netherlands.

Japan, January 30, 1856, October 16, 1857; Sandwich Islands, October 16, 1862; Liberia, December 20, 1862; Venezuela, March 21, 1872; Orange Free States, November 14, 1874; Switzerland, June 18, 1875, August 24, 1877; Morocco, July 3, 1880.

Portugal.

China, August 13, 1862; Transvaal, December 11, 1875; Great Britain, December 11, 1875; Morocco, July 3, 1880.

Russia.

Austria, November 8, 1847; Denmark, May 25, 1850; Japan, January 26, 1855; Turkey, March 30, 1856; Austria, etc., March 30, 1856; Great Britain, March 30, 1856; China, June 13, 1858; Turkey, August 19, 1858; Bavaria, August 22, 1866; Turkey, February 8, 1879.

Moldo-Wallachia.

Austria, February 19, 1858.

Montenegro.

Great Britain, January 22, 1882.

Servia.

France, January 18, 1863, January 18, 1883; Great Britain, February 7, 1880; United States, May 2–14, 1881.

Spain.

Persia, March 4, 1842; Costa Rica, May 10, 1850; Morocco, April 26, 1860; Annam, June 5, 1862; Peru, January 27, 1865, August 14, 1879; Morocco, July 3, 1880; Chile, January 12, 1853; Great Britain, December 1, 1883.

Sweden and Norway.

China, March 20, 1847; Morocco, July 3, 1880.

Switzerland.

United States, November 25, 1850; Great Britain, September 6, 1855; Persia, July 23, 1873; Denmark, February 13, 1875; Netherlands, July 18, 1875; Salvador, October 30, 1883.

Turkey.

France, March 30, 1856, August 19, 1858; Great Britain, March 30, 1856, August 19, 1858; Germany, August 19, 1858; Italy, August 19, 1858; Russia, August 19, 1858, October 16, 1862, February 8, 1879.

ASIATIC STATES.

Afghanistan.

Great Britain, July 23, 1855, March 26, 1879.

Annam.

France, June 5, 1862, March 15, 1874.

Burmah.

Italy, March 3, 1871; France, January 24, 1873.

China.

United States, July 8, 1844; Sweden, March 20, 1847; Russia, June 13, 1858; France, June 27, 1858, October 25, 1860; Portugal, October 13, 1862; Austria, September 2, 1869; Japan, August 30, 1871; Peru, June 26, 1874.

Corea.

Great Britain, February 21, 1860, November 26, 1883; Japan, November 24, 1876; Germany, November 26, 1883.

Japan.

Russia, January 26, 1855; Netherlands, January 30, 1856, August 16, 1857; Great Britain, August 26, 1858; France, October 9, 1859; Germany, February 20, 1869; Austria, October 18, 1869; China, August 30, 1871; Corea, August 24, 1876.

Persia.

Belgium, July 14, 1841; Spain, March 4, 1842; United States, December 13, 1856; Great Britain, March 4, 1857; Denmark, November 30, 1857; Switzerland, July 23, 1873.

Samoa.

United States, June 17, 1878; Germany, January 24, 1879; Great Britain, August 28, 1879.

Siam.

Great Britain, April 18, 1855; France, August 15, 1856; Denmark, May 21, 1858; Austria, May 17, 1869.

AFRICAN STATES.

Ashanti.

Great Britain, February 13, 1874.

Hawaii.

Austria, June 18, 1875; Germany, March 25, 1879; Great Britain, July 10, 1851.

Borneo.

Great Britain, May 21, 1847.

Liberia.

Great Britain, November 21, 1848; Netherlands, December 20, 1862; North Germany, October 31, 1867.

Madagascar.

Great Britain, June 27, 1865; France, September 12, 1862, August 8, 1868; United States, May 13, 1881; Germany, May 15, 1883.

Morocco.

Great Britain, December 9, 1856, July 3, 1880; Spain, April 26, 1860; Germany, etc., July 3, 1880; Belgium, July 3, 1880; Denmark, July 3, 1880; France, July 3, 1880; Italy, July 3, 1880; Netherlands, July 3, 1880; Portugal, July 3, 1880.

Orange Free States.

Belgium, April 1, 1874; Netherlands, November 14, 1876.

Sandwich Islands.

France, October 29, 1857; Netherlands, October 16, 1862.

Tonga.

Germany, November 1, 1875; Great Britain, November 29, 1879.

Transvaal.

Belgium, December 11, 1875; Portugal, December 11, 1875; Great Britain, February 27, 1884.

Republic of South Africa.

Germany, January 22, 1885.

Zanzibar.

Great Britain, April 30, 1886.

AMERICAN STATES.

Argentine Confederation.

Great Britain, November 24, 1849; Germany, September 15, 1857; Paraguay, February 3, 1876.

Bolivia.

Brazil, March 27, 1867.

Brazil.

Uruguay, October, 12, 1851; Bolivia, March 27, 1867; Paraguay, January 9, 1872.

Chile.

France, October 7, 1849; North Germany, February 1, 1862; Spain, June 12, 1883; Peru, October 20, 1883.

Colombia.

Equator, December 30, 1863; Great Britain, February 16, 1866.

Costa Rica.

Great Britain, November 27, 1849; Spain, May 10, 1850; Germany, May 18, 1875.

Dominica.

Great Britain, March 6, 1850.

Equator.

Great Britain, May 3, 1851, October 18, 1880; Colombia, December 30, 1863.

Guatemala.

France, March 8, 1848; Great Britain, February 20, 1849; Belgium, March 27, 1849.

Honduras.

France, February 22, 1856; Great Britain, August 27, 1856.

Mexico.

United States, February 2, 1848; North Germany, August 28, 1869, December 5, 1882; United States, January 20, 1883.

New Grenada.

United States, December 12, 1846; Sardinia, August 18, 1847.

Nicaragua.

Belgium, March 27, 1849; Spain, July 25, 1850; France, April 11, 1859; Great Britain, February 11, 1860.

Paraguay.

United States, February 4, 1859; North Germany, August 1, 1860; Brazil, January 9, 1872; Argentine Republic, February 3, 1876; Uruguay, August 20, 1883; Great Britain, October 16, 1884.

Peru.

Great Britain, April 10, 1850; Belgium, May 16, 1850; United States, July 22, 1856, September 6, 1870; Spain, February 27, 1865; China, June 26, 1874; Spain, August 14, 1879; Chile, October 20, 1883.

Salvador.

France, January 2, 1858; Great Britain, October 24, 1862; Germany, June 13, 1870; Switzerland, October 30, 1883.

San Domingo.

Hayti, July 26, 1867.

United States.

China, July 8, 1844; New Grenada, December 12, 1846; Mexico, February 2, 1848; Austria, May 8, 1848; Hawaii, December 20, 1849; Borneo, January 23, 1850; Switzerland, November 25, 1850; Two Sicilies, January 10, 1855; Persia, December 13, 1856; Paraguay, February 4, 1859; Peru, September 7, 1870; Orange Free States, December 22, 1871; Samoa, January 17, 1878; Morocco, July 3, 1880; Madagascar, May 13, 1881; Servia, May 2-14, 1883.

Uruguay.

Great Britain, August 26, 1842; France, August 18, 1873; Paraguay, August 20, 1883.

Venezuela.

Netherlands, March 21, 1872.

CHAPTER X.

SECTION I.

AMBASSADORS AND OTHER DIPLOMATIC AGENTS.

183. STATES have the right to appoint Ambassadors, Ministers, and other Diplomatic Agents, to reside with their families and establishments permanently at each other's capital, or to visit it occasionally, at the option of either Government.

184. Ambassadors or Ministers ought not to be called upon to perform any ceremony derogatory to their character as representing the Sovereigns of independent States. They have the right to use the same forms of ceremony and respect to the Sovereigns they are sent to, as are employed by the same Ambassadors, Ministers, or Diplomatic Agents towards any Sovereign of independent and equal States.

185. States have also the right to acquire a site for building, or to hire houses for the accommodation of their missions. Their representatives have the right to choose their own servants and attendants, the same being subjected to no molestation whatever. Any person being guilty of disrespect or violence to such Representatives or any member of their families or establishments, in deed or word, should be severely punished.

186. No obstacle or difficulty must be made to the free movements of such Representatives, and they and the persons of their suite have the right to come and go and travel at their pleasure. They have, moreover, full liberty to send and receive their correspondence; and their letters and effects are to be held sacred and inviolable. They may employ, for their transmission, special couriers, who ought to meet with the same protection and facilities for travelling as the persons employed in carrying despatches for the Imperial Government; and generally they are to enjoy the same privileges as are accorded to officers of the same rank by the usage and consent of Western nations.

SECTION II.

CONSULS.

187. States are at liberty to appoint Consuls for the protection of trade, to reside in the dominions and territories of the other party; but before any Consul can act as such, he must, in the usual form, be approved and admitted by the Government to which he is sent, and either of the contracting parties may except from the residence of Consuls such particular places as either of them may judge fit to be so excepted.

188. The Consuls-General, Consuls, Vice-Consuls, and Consular Agents of each of the contracting parties, residing in the territories and possessions of the other, have the right to exercise the functions pertaining to their office, with which they may be charged by their Government, without prejudice to the laws and regulations of the country of their residence; and, in like manner, they enjoy the privileges, exemptions, and immunities permitted by the same laws and regulations.

189. The Consuls-General, Consuls, Vice-Consuls, and Consular Agents of each of the

contracting parties, residing in the territories of
the other, have a right to receive from the local
authorities such assistance as can by law be
given to them for the recovery of deserters from
the vessels of their respective countries.

190. Should a subject of one of the contracting parties die within the dominions of the
other, and should there be no person present at
the time of such death rightly entitled to administer to the estate of such deceased person,
the following rules are observed :—

191. When the deceased leaves, in the above-
named circumstances, heirs of his own nationality only, or who may be qualified to enjoy
the civil status of their father, the Consuls-
General, Consuls, Vice-Consuls, or Consular
Agents of the nation to which the deceased
belonged, giving notice to the proper authorities,
shall take possession and have custody of the
property of the said deceased, shall pay the expenses of the funeral, and retain the surplus for
the payment of the debts, and for the benefit of
the heirs to whom it may rightfully belong.

192. But the said Consuls-General, Consuls,

Vice-Consuls, or other Consular Agents are bound immediately to apply to the proper court for Letters of Administration of the effects left by the deceased, and these letters are delivered to him with such limitations and for such time as to such court may seem right.

193. If, however, the deceased leaves, in the country of his decease, and in the above-named circumstances, any heir or universal legatee of other nationality than his own, or to whom the civil status of their fathers cannot be granted, then each of the two Governments may determine whether the proper court shall proceed according to law, or shall confide the collection and administration to the respective Consular functionaries under the proper limitations.

194. Where there is no Consul-General, Consul, Vice-Consul, or Consular Agent in the locality where the decease has occurred (in the case contemplated by the first rule of this article), upon whom devolve the custody and administration of the estate, the proper authority proceeds in these acts, until the arrival of the respective Consular functionary.

Respecting Consular Jurisdiction, the Treaty be-
tween Great Britain and China of August 23, 1842,
and June 26, 1858, as well as the Treaty with Japan,
August 26, 1858, provided as follows:—

195. Whenever a British subject has reason
to complain of a native, he must first proceed
to the Consulate and state his grievance; the
Consul will thereupon inquire into the merits of
the case, and do his utmost to arrange it amicably.
In like manner, if a native have reason to complain of a British subject, he shall no less listen
to his complaint and endeavour to settle it in a
friendly manner.

196. If an English merchant have occasion
to address the national authorities, he shall send
such address through the Consul, who will see
that the language is becoming; and if otherwise,
he will direct it to be changed or will refuse to
convey the address.

197. If unfortunately any dispute takes place
of such a nature that the Consul cannot arrange
it amicably, then he shall request the assistance of a native officer, that they may together

examine into the merits of the case and decide it equitably.

198. All questions in regard to rights, whether of property or person, arising between British subjects in China or Japan are subject to the jurisdiction of the British authorities.

199. Chinese or Japanese subjects who may be guilty of any criminal act towards British subjects shall be arrested and punished by the Chinese or Japanese authorities according to the laws of China or Japan.

200. British subjects who may commit any crime against Chinese or Japanese subjects or the subjects or citizens of any other country shall be tried and punished by the Consul or other public functionary authorized thereto according to the laws of Great Britain.

201. Justice shall be equitably and impartially administered on both sides.

See British Treaties with Morocco, December 9, 1856; *China, June* 26, 1858; *Japan, August* 26, 1858; *Afghanistan, May* 26, 1879; *Servia, February* 7, 1880; *Corea, November* 26, 1883; *South African Republic, February* 27, 1884.

Treaties concerning the Appointment of Diplomatic Agents and Consuls.

European States.

Austria.

United States, July 11, 1870; Portugal, January 9, 1873; Italy, May 15, 1874; Servia, May 6, 1881.

Belgium.

Spain, March 19, 1870; Italy, July 22, 1878; United States, March 9, 1880; Roumania, January 12, 1881; Servia, January 7–15, 1885.

France.

Brazil, December 10, 1860; Italy, July 26, 1862; Russia, April 1, 1874; Greece, January 7, 1876; Salvador, July 5, 1878.

Great Britain.

United States, July 3, 1818; Buenos Ayres, February 2, 1825; Venezuela, April 18, 1825; Mexico, December 26, 1826; Greece, October 11, 1837; Peru, June 5, 1837, April 16, 1850; Muscat, May 31, 1839; Persia, October 28, 1841, March 4, 1857; Abyssinia, November 2, 1849; Liberia, November 21, 1848; Dominica, March 6, 1850; Johanna, June 3, 1850; Equator, May 3, 1851; Sandwich Islands, July 10, 1851; Siam, April 18, 1855, May 13, 1856; Switzerland, September 6, 1855; Russia, March 30, 1856, June 12, 1859; Morocco, December 9, 1856; Japan, August 26, 1858; China, June 26, 1858; Salvador, October 24, 1862; Italy, August 6, 1863; Madagascar, June 27, 1865; Columbia, February 16, 1866; Brazil, April 22, 1873; Zanzibar, April 30, 1886.

Germany and Prussia.

Netherlands, June 16, 1856; Italy, December 21, 1868, February 7, 1872; Spain, February 22, 1870; United States, December 11, 1871; Russia, December 8, 1875; Greece, November 20, 1881; Brazil, January 10, 1882; Servia, January 6, 1883.

Greece.

Great Britain, October 11, 1837; France, January 7, 1876; Germany, November 20, 1881.

Italy.

France, July 26, 1862 ; Peru, May 3, 1863 ; Great Britain, August 6, 1863 ; Portugal, September 30, 1868, July 16, 1875 ; Germany, December 21, 1868, February 7, 1872 ; Guatemala, January 2, 1873 ; Turkey, February 24, 1873 ; Austria, May 15, 1874 ; Russia, April 28, 1875 ; Netherlands, August 3, 1875 ; Salvador, July 25, 1876 ; Brazil, August 6, 1876 ; Belgium, July 22, 1878 ; Switzerland, July 28, 1879 ; United States, May 8, 1878 ; Servia, November 9, 1879.

Netherlands.

Prussia, June 16, 1856 ; United States, May 23, 1858 ; Brazil, September 27, 1858 ; Italy, August 3, 1875 ; Spain, November 18, 1871, February 10, 1873 ; Portugal, December 1, 1880 ; Russia, April 14, 1883 ; Hayti, May 18, 1883.

Portugal.

Italy, September 30, 1868, July 16, 1875 ; Austria, January 9, 1873 ; Netherlands, December 1, 1880.

Roumania.

Switzerland, February 14, 1880 ; Belgium, January 12, 1881.

Russia.

Great Britain, March 30, 1856, June 12, 1859 ; France, April 1, 1874 ; Germany, December 8, 1875 ; Italy, April 28, 1875 ; Spain, February 23, 1876 ; Netherlands, April 14, 1883 ; United States, May 25, 1884.

Servia.

Italy, November 9, 1879 ; Austria, May 6, 1881 ; United States, October 2-15, 1881 ; Germany, January 6, 1883 ; Belgium, January 7-15, 1885.

Spain.

Italy, July 26, 1862 ; Spain, February 22, 1870 ; Belgium, March 19, 1870 ; Netherlands, November 18, 1871, February 10, 1873 ; Russia, February 23, 1876.

Switzerland.

Great Britain, September 6, 1855 ; Brazil, October 12, 1878 ; Italy, January 28, 1879 ; Roumania, February 14, 1880.

Turkey.

Italy, February 24, 1873.

AMERICAN STATES.

Brazil.

Netherlands, September 27, 1858; France, December 10, 1860; Great Britain, April 22, 1873; Italy, August 6, 1876; Netherlands, May 8, 1878; Switzerland, October 12, 1878; Germany, January 10, 1882.

Buenos Ayres.

Great Britain, February 2, 1825.

Colombia.

Great Britain, February 16, 1866.

Dominica.

Great Britain, March 6, 1850.

Equator.

Great Britain, May 3, 1851.

Guatemala.

Italy, January 2, 1873.

Hayti.

Netherlands, May 18, 1883.

Mexico.

Great Britain, December 6, 1826.

Peru.

Great Britain, June 5, 1837, April 16, 1850; Italy, May 3, 1863.

Salvador.

Great Britain, October 24, 1862; United States, December 6, 1870; Italy, January 7, 1876; France, July 5, 1878.

Sandwich Islands.

Great Britain, July 10, 1851.

United States.

Great Britain, July 3, 1818; Netherlands, May 23, 1858; Austria, July 11, 1870; Salvador, December 6, 1871; Germany, December 11, 1871; Italy, May 8, 1878; Belgium, March 9, 1880; Servia, October 2–15, 1881; Russia, May 25, 1884.

Venezuela.

Great Britain, April 18, 1825.

AFRICAN STATES.

Johanna.

Great Britain, June 3, 1850.

Liberia.

Great Britain, November 28, 1848.

Madagascar.

Great Britain, June 27, 1865.

Morocco.

Great Britain, December 9, 1856.

Muscat.

Great Britain, May 31, 1839.

Zanzibar.

Great Britain, April 30, 1866.

ASIATIC STATES.

China.

Great Britain, June 26, 1858.

Japan.

Great Britain, August 28, 1858.

Persia.

Great Britain, November 2, 1849.

Siam.

Great Britain, April 18, 1855, May 13, 1856.

CHAPTER XI.

TREATY CLAUSES CONCERNING COMMERCE AND NAVIGATION.

202. THE right to trade, itself an imperfect right, may be perfected by Treaties.

203. States have a right to trade with each other's dominions and possessions, and to enjoy the same rights, privileges, liberty, favours, immunities, and exemptions in matters of commerce and navigation which are or may be enjoyed by native subjects, the subjects of each contracting party conforming themselves to the laws of the country.

204. Under "the most favoured clause," no higher or other duties can be imposed on the importation into the dominion of one party of any article the growth, produce, or manufacture

of the other, and no higher or other duties can
be imposed on the importation into one country
of any article the growth, produce, or manufacture of the other, than are or shall be payable
on the same or the like articles, being the produce
or manufacture of any other foreign country.
And no higher or other duty or charges can be
imposed on either of the two countries on the
exportation of any article to the territories of
the other than such as are payable on the ex- .
portation of the same or the like article to any
other foreign country.

205. No prohibition can be imposed upon
the importation of any article the growth, produce, or manufacture of the territories of either
of the contracting parties into the territories of
the other which shall not equally extend to the
importation of the same or the like article, being
the growth, produce, or manufacture of any other
country ; and no prohibition can be imposed on
the exportation of any article from the territories
of either of the contracting parties to the territories of the other, which shall not equally extend
to the exportation of the same or the like article
to the territories of all other nations.

206. No duties of tonnage, harbour, pilotage, lighthouse, quarantine, or other similar or corresponding duties, of whatever nature or under whatever denomination, levied in the name of the Government, public functionaries, corporations, or establishments of whatever kind, can be imposed in the ports of either country which shall not be equally imposed in the like cases upon national vessels.

207. The subjects of both contracting parties have the right to carry on their commerce by wholesale or by retail, and either in person or by any agent whom they may think fit to employ.

208. They are not subject in respect of their persons or property, or in respect of passports, licences for residence or establishment, or in respect of their commerce or industry, to any taxes, whether general or local, nor to imposts or obligations of any kind whatever, other or greater than those which are or may be imposed upon native subjects.

209. They enjoy in the dominions and possessions of each other equality of treatment with native subjects in regard to loading and un-

loading, to warehousing, and to the transit trade, as also in regard to bounties, facilities, etc.

210. They have the same rights as native subjects as regard the patents for inventions, trade marks, and designs, upon fulfilment of the formalities prescribed by law.

211. All vessels which according to the laws of each contracting party are to be deemed national vessels, or vessels belonging to the subjects of that State, shall also be respectively deemed national vessels, and vessels belonging to the subjects of the same.

212. If any ship of war or merchant vessel of one of the contracting parties should run aground or be wrecked, or meet with any casualty upon the coast of the other, the same aid or assistance must be rendered to it, and to the cargo, apparel, and furniture thereof, as to a national vessel; and in such a case no other expense is to be paid by the owners or their agents and representatives for the preservation of the property, or of the lives of the persons on board the ship, than would be payable in the like case of a wreck or casualty to a national vessel.

213. In case the master of a merchant vessel should be under the necessity of disposing of part of his merchandise in order to defray any salvage expenses, no impediment shall be offered by the authorities, the master being bound to conform to the existing regulations and tariffs.

214. Goods and merchandise saved from the wreck are to be exempt from all duties of customs, unless cleared for consumption.

215. If a seaman of one of the contracting parties, after serving on board a ship of the other contracting State, should remain behind in a third State, or in its Colonies, or in the Colonies of that State whose flag the ship carries, and the said seaman is in a helpless condition in consequence of shipwreck, or from other causes, then the Government of the State whose flag the ship bears shall be bound to support the said seaman until he enters into the ship's service again, or find other employment, or until he arrives in his native State or its Colonies, or dies.

216. Such assistance shall, however, be granted on condition that the seaman so situated shall

avail himself of the first opportunity that offers to prove his necessitous condition and the causes thereof to the proper officials of the State whose support is to be solicited, and that the destitution is shown to be the natural consequence of the termination of his service on board the ship, otherwise the aforesaid liability to afford relief lapses.

217. The said liability is also excluded if the seaman has deserted, or has been turned out of the ship for any criminal act, or left it on account of disability for service in consequence of illness or wounding resulting from his own fault. The relief includes maintenance, clothing, medical attendance, medicine, travelling expenses ; in case of death the funeral expenses are also to be paid.

The following Treaties on Commerce and Navigation have been concluded since 1840 :—

EUROPEAN STATES.

Austria and Austria-Hungary.

Netherlands, December 29, 1856; Persia, December 17, 1857; Great Britain, April 30, 1868, December 5, 1876 ; Portugal, January 13, 1872 ; Sweden, November 3, 1873, November 26, 1873; Roumania, June 22, 1875 ; Germany, December 16, 1878; Spain, July 2, 1880; France, February 18, 1883.

Belgium.

United States, July 12, 1858; Prussia, March 28, 1863; Netherlands, May 12, 1863; Germany, May 22, 1865; Spain, February 12, 1870, June 5, 1875; France, July 23, 1873, October 31, 1881, July 31, 1882; Portugal, February 23, 1874; Chile, June 5, 1875; Spain, May 4, 1878; Roumania, August 14, 1880; Venezuela, March 1, 1884; Servia, March 7-15, 1885.

Denmark.

Switzerland, May 22, 1875.

France.

New Grenada, May 15, 1856, January 27, 1857; Russia, June 25, 1857; Great Britain, January 23, 1860, July 23, 1873, January 22, 1874; Turkey, April 29, 1860; Belgium, April 29, 1860, July 23, 1873; Germany, August 2, 1862; Belgium, October 31, 1881, January 31, 1882; Portugal, December 19, 1881, May 6, 1882; Sweden and Norway, December 30, 1881; Switzerland, February 20, 1882; Austria, February 18, 1883.

Germany.

Mexico, July 10, 1855; Uruguay, June 25, 1856; Persia, June 25, 1857, June 6, 1872; Great Britain, November 11, 1857; China, September 2, 1861, May 30, 1865; Turkey, March 20, 1862; France, August 2, 1862; Belgium, March 28, 1863, May 22, 1865; Great Britain, May 30, 1865; Spain, March 30, 1868, July 2, 1883; Switzerland, May 13, 1869; Portugal, March 9, 1872; Italy, November 28, 1872; Austria, December 16, 1878; Servia, January 6, 1883; Greece, July 9, 1884; Dominican Republic, January 30, 1885; Zanzibar, December 20, 1885.

Great Britain.

Switzerland, December 6, 1855; Morocco, December 9, 1856; Germany, November 11, 1857, May 30, 1865; Russia, January 12, 1859; France, January 23, 1860, July 23, 1873, January 22, 1874, February 24, 1882; Austria, April 30, 1868, December 5, 1878, November 26, 1877; Siam, January 14, 1874; Portugal, December 20, 1878, March 8, 1879, May 22, 1882; Roumania, April 5, 1880; Italy, July 15, 1883; Egypt, March 3, 1884; Greece, November 10, 1886.

The following Treaties of Commerce and Navigation between Great Britain and Foreign Powers are now in force, containing most favoured nation clauses (see list presented to Parliament, 1883) :—

Argentine Confederation ...	February 2, 1825, commerce and navigation.
„ „ ...	July 10, 1858, free navigation, Parana-Uruguay.
Austria	April 30, 1868, navigation.
Austria-Hungary	December 5, 1876, commerce.
Belgium	July 23, 1862, commerce and navigation.
„	August 30, 1862, cotton yarn.
„	November 13, 1862, commerce and navigation.
Bolivia	September 29, 1840, commerce and navigation.
Borneo	May 27, 1847, ditto.
Chile	October 4, 1854, ditto.
China	June 26, 1858, ditto.
Colombia	February 16, 1866, ditto
Corea	November 26, 1883, friendship and commerce.
Costa Rica	November 27, 1849, ditto.
Denmark	February 13, 1862, ditto.
Dominica	March 6, 1850, ditto.
„	September 7, 1860, ditto.
Egypt	March 3, 1884, most favoured nation.
Equador	May 3, 1851, ditto.
„	October 18, 1880, ditto.
France	January 26, 1826, ditto.
„	February 28, 1882, commercial and maritime.
Germany	May 30, 1865, commerce.
Greece	October 4, 1837, commerce and navigation; November 10, 1886.
Italy	June 15, 1883, ditto.

Japan ...	...	...	October 14, 1854, ditto.
„ ...	...	...	May 26, 1858, ditto.
Liberia ...	...	...	November 21, 1848, ditto.
Madagascar...	...	...	June 27, 1865, ditto.
„ ...	...	...	February 16, 1883, holding of land by British subjects.
„ ...	...	...	May 25, 1883, traffic in spiritous liquors.
Montenegro	...	...	January 21, 1843, commerce and navigation.
„	...	...	January 21, 1882, interior tax on sales of goods.
Morocco ...	...	...	December 9, 1856, general treaty.
„ ...	...	...	December 9, 1886, commerce and navigation.
Muscat ...	...	...	May 31, 1839, ditto.
Netherlands	...	...	March 17, 1824, commercial inter-course colonies.
„ ...	...	...	October 27, 1837, commerce and navigation.
„ ...	...	...	March 27, 1851, ditto.
„ ...	...	...	March 6, 1856, consuls in colonies.
Nicaragua ...	...	...	February 11, 1860, commerce and navigation.
Paraguay ...	...	...	October 16, 1884, friendship, com-merce, and navigation.
Persia ...	...	...	October 28, 1861, ditto.
„ ...	...	...	March 6, 1857, ditto.
Peru ...	...	...	April 10, 1850, ditto.
Portugal ...	...	...	July 3, 1842, ditto.
„ ...	...	...	May 22, 1882, commerce, etc.
Prussia ...	...	...	August 16, 1865, commerce and navigation.
Roumania ...	...	...	April 5, 1880, ditto.
„ ...	...	...	April 5, 1880, non-application of Treaty of 1880 to South African colonies.
„ ...	...	...	January $\frac{7}{12}$, 1881, non-application of Treaty to Canada.

Russia	...	...	January 12, 1859, commerce and navigation.
Salvador	...	...	October 24, 1862, ditto.
Samoa	...	...	August 28, 1879, commerce.
Sandwich Islands ...		...	July 10, 1881, commerce and navigation.
Servia	...	...	February 7, 1880, commerce.
„	...	...	February 7, 1880, Servian frontier traffic.
„	...	...	July 4, 1881, commerce and non-application of Treaty of 1880 to Canada and South African colonies.
Siam	...	...	April 18, 1855, commerce.
„	...	...	April 6, 1883, traffic in spirituous liquors.
Spain	...	...	May 23, 1667, commerce and navigation.
„	...	...	July 13, 1713, ditto.
„	...	...	December 9, 1713, ditto.
„	...	...	December 14, 1715, ditto.
„	...	...	October 5, 1750, ditto.
„	...	...	July 5, 1814, ditto.
„	...	...	August 28, 1814, ditto.
„	...	...	April 26, 1886, commercial relations.
Sweden and Norway		...	March 18, 1826, commerce and navigation.
Switzerland	...	...	September 6, 1855, commerce and residence.
Tonga	...	...	November 29, 1879, friendship.
Tunis	...	...	October 10, 1863, commerce, etc.
„	...	...	July 19, 1879, ditto.
Turkey	...	...	April 29, 1861, commerce and navigation.
United States	...	...	July 3, 1815, ditto.
„		...	October 20, 1818, ditto.
„		...	August 6, 1827, ditto.
Venezuela	...	...	April 18, 1825, ditto.
„	...	...	October 29, 1834, ditto.

Greece.

Egypt, March 3, 1881; Germany, July 9, 1884; Great Britain, November 10, 1886.

Italy.

Netherlands, November 24, 1863; United States, February 26, 1871; Germany, November 28, 1872, May 4, 1883; Russia, December 26, 1872, September 16, 1876; Peru, December 20, 1874; Austria, December 27, 1878; Portugal, July 15, 1882; Belgium, December 11, 1882; Switzerland, March 22, 1883; Montenegro, March 28, 1883.

Montenegro.

Italy, March 28, 1873.

Netherlands.

Japan, November 9, 1855, January 30, 1856, October 16, 1857; Austria, December 29, 1855; Tunis, January 17, 1856; Turkey, February 23, 1862; Belgium, May 12, 1863; Italy, November 24, 1863, May 22, 1876; Spain, November 18, 1871; Portugal December 20, 1874, April 24, 1875.

Portugal.

Great Britain, July 3, 1842, December 26, 1878, May 22, 1882; Austria, January 13, 1872; Italy, July 25, 1872; Switzerland, December 6, 1873; Belgium, February 23, 1874; Netherlands, January 3, 1875, April 24, 1875; France, December 19, 1881, May 6, 1882.

Roumania.

Austria, June 22, 1875; Russia, March 27, 1876; Germany, November 14, 1877; Great Britain, April 5, 1880; Belgium, August 14, 1880; Netherlands, June 17, 1881.

Servia.

Austria, February 22, 1882; Germany, January 6, 1883; Belgium, March 7–15, 1885.

Spain.

Germany, March 30, 1868, November 14, 1877, July 12, 1883; Belgium, February 12, 1870; Italy, February 22, 1870, June 23, 1875; Sweden and Norway, February 28, 1871; Netherlands,

November 18, 1871; Russia, February 23, 1876; France, February 6, 1882.

Sweden and Norway.

Spain, February 25, 1871; Austria, November 3, 1873 ; France, December 30, 1881.

Switzerland.

Great Britain, September 6, 1855; Germany, May 13, 1869, May 23, 1881, May 4, 1883; Russia, December 26, 1872; Portugal, December 6, 1873; Denmark, May 22, 1875 ; Italy, March 22, 1883 ; Spain, May 14, 1883.

Turkey.

France, April 29, 1860; Netherlands, February 23, 1862 ; Germany, March 20, 1863.

ASIATIC STATES.

Annam.

France, August 31, 1874.

Bokhara.

Russia, February 10, 1868.

China.

Germany, September 2, 1861.

Japan.

Netherlands, November 9, 1855, December 30, 1856, October 16, 1857; United States, July 29, 1858, July 25, 1878.

Persia.

Germany, June 25, 1857, June 6, 1874 ; Austria, December 17, 1857.

Siam.

United States, May 29, 1856; Great Britain, January 14, 1874.

African States.

Egypt.

Greece, March 3, 1884.

Tunis.

Austria, January 17, 1856.

Zanzibar.

Germany, December 20, 1885.

American States.

Brazil.

Paraguay, January 18, 1872, April 30, 1874.

Chile.

Belgium, June 5, 1875.

Dominican Republic.

Germany, January 30, 1885.

Hawaii.

United States, January 30, 1875.

Mexico.

Germany, July 10, 1855; Italy, December 14, 1870; United States, January 20, 1883.

New Grenada.

France, January 27, 1857, May 15, 1876.

Paraguay.

Brazil, January 18, 1872, April 30, 1874.

Peru.

Russia, May 16, 1874; Italy, December 20, 1874.

United States.

Two Sicilies, October 1, 1855; Siam, May 29, 1856; Japan, July 17, 1858, July 25, 1858; Belgium, July 17, 1858; Italy, February 26, 1871; Hawaii, January 30, 1875; Mexico, January 20, 1883.

Venezuela.

Belgium, March 1, 1884.

CHAPTER XII

218. STATES have an exclusive right of fishery within the distance of three miles from low-water mark along the whole extent of their coasts.

219. The mile is a geographical mile, whereof sixty make a degree of latitude.

The following are special Treaties on the subject of fisheries :—

Convention between Great Britain and France, November 11, 1867.

" I. British fishermen shall enjoy the exclusive right of fishery within the distance of three miles from low-water mark along the whole extent of the coasts of the British Islands, and French fishermen shall enjoy the exclusive right of fishery within the distance of three miles from low-water mark along the whole extent of the coast of France, the only

exception to this rule being that part of the coast of
France which lies between Cape Carteret and Point
Meinga. The distance of three miles fixed as the
general limit for the exclusive right of fishery upon
the coast of the two countries, shall, with respect to
bays, the mouths of which do not exceed ten miles in
width, be measured from a straight line drawn from
headland to headland. The miles mentioned in the
present Convention are geographical miles, whereof
sixty make a degree of latitude.

" III. The arrangements of the Convention shall
apply beyond the fishery limits of both Countries as
defined by the same in the seas surrounding and
adjoining Great Britain and Ireland, and adjoining
the Coasts of France between the frontiers of Belgium
and Spain. The rules respecting Oyster fishery shall,
however, be observed only in the seas comprised
within the limits thereafter defined.

"X. Fishing of all kinds, by whatever means and
at all seasons, may be carried on in the seas lying
beyond the fishery limits which have been fixed for
the two Countries, with the exception of that for
Oysters as thereafter expressed.

"XXIV. All infractions of the regulations concerning the placing of boats on the fishery grounds,
the distance to be observed between them, the prohibition of oyster fishing during a portion of the year,
and concerning every other operation connected with
the act of fishing, and more particularly concerning

circumstance likely to cause damage, shall be taken cognizance of by the cruisers of either nation, which-ever may be the nation to which the fishermen guilty of such infractions may belong.

"XXXI. Fishing boats of either of the two countries shall be admitted to sell their fish in such parts of the other country as may be designated for that purpose, on condition that they conform to the regulations mutually agreed upon.

"XXXII. The fishing boats of the one country shall not enter within the fishery limits fixed for the other country, except under the following circum-stances :—

"1. When driven by stress of weather or by evident damage.

"2. When carried in by contrary winds, by strong tides, or by any other cause beyond the control of master and crew.

"3. When obliged by contrary winds or tide to beat up in order to reach their fishing ground, and when, from the same cause of contrary wind or tide, they could not, if they remained outside, be able to hold on their course to their fishing ground.

"4. When during the herring fishing season the herring boats of the one country shall find it neces-sary to anchor under shelter of the coasts of the other country, in order to await the opportunity for pro-ceeding to their fishing ground.

"5. When proceeding to any of the ports of the

other country open to them for the sale of fish in accordance with the preceding article; but in such case they shall never have oyster dredges on board.

"The Convention shall continue in force for ten years from the day on which it may come into operation, and subsequently from year to year."

Convention regarding the Newfoundland Fisheries.

By the Treaty of Utrecht of 1713, whilst the Island called Newfoundland was ceded by the French to Britain, the French were allowed to catch fish and to dry them on land in that part only, and in no other besides that, of the said island which stretches from the place called Cape Bonavista to the northern point of the Island and from thence, running down by the western side, reaches as far as the place called Point Riche.

By Art. V. of the Treaty of Paris of 1763, after renewing the above provisions regarding liberty of the French to fish and dry on a part of the coast of Newfoundland, liberty was given to the French to fish on the Gulf of St. Lawrence at the distance of three leagues from the coast, and on the coast of the Island of Cape Breton at the distance of fifteen leagues from the coast, the Islands of St. Pierre and Miquelon being left to France to serve as a shelter to the French fishermen. By the Treaty of Versailles of 1783, France renounced the right of fishing from Cape Bonavista to

Cape St. John, and Britain consented that the French fishery should extend on the western coast of Newfoundland to the place called Cape Ray, situate in 67° 50′ latitude.

Arrangement signed at Paris, November 14, 1885.

"Art. 1. The Government of Her Majesty the Queen of the United Kingdom engages to comply with the following regulations for securing to French fishermen, in execution of the treaties in force, and particularly of the Declaration of 1783, the free exercise of their industry on the Coast of Newfoundland, without any interference or obstruction whatever on the part of British subjects.

"Art. 2. The Government of the French Republic engages on its part, in exchange for the security accorded to French fishermen by the application of the regulations contained in the present arrangement, not to raise any objections against the formation of establishments necessary for the development of every industry other than that of the fisheries on those portions of the coasts of Newfoundland comprised between Cape St. John and Cape Ray.

"It engages equally not to disturb the resident British subjects in respect of the establishment actually existing on those parts of the coast comprised between Cape St. John and Cape Ray passing by the North, but no new ones will be established on

9

those parts of the coast described in the statement mentioned in the preceding paragraph.

"Art. 3. Notwithstanding the prohibition stipulated at the end of the second paragraph of the preceding article, in the case where a mine should be discovered in the vicinity of any one of the coasts comprised in the statement annexed to the present arrangement, the Government of the French Republic engages not to raise any objection to the persons interested enjoying, for the working of such mine, facilities compatible with the free exercise of the French fisheries.

"Art. 4. It is understood that French citizens shall retain in full, on all those parts of the coast comprised between Cape St. John and Cape Ray, the right as it is defined by treaty of fishing or drying and curing their fish, etc., as well as of cutting wood, in all parts, except on enclosed property, necessary for fishing stages, huts, and fishing boats.

"Art. 15. The French Government abandons for its subjects the salmon fisheries in rivers, and only reserves a right to the salmon fishing in the sea and at the mouth of rivers up to the point where the water remains salt; but it is forbidden to place fixed barriers capable of impeding interior navigation or the circulation of the fish.

"Art. 16. French fishermen shall be exempt from the payment of any duties on the importation into that part of the Island of Newfoundland comprised between Cape St. John and Cape Ray, passing by the north, of all articles, goods, provisions, etc., which are necessary for the prosecution of their fishing industry, for their subsistence, and for their temporary establishment on the coast of this British possession.

" They shall also be exempt on the same part of the coast from the payment of all light and port dues and other shipping dues.

" Art. 17. French fishermen shall have the right to purchase bait, both herring and capelin, on shore or at sea, on the shores of Newfoundland, free from all duty or restrictions, subsequent to the 5th of April in each year and up to the close of the fishing season."

Convention between Great Britain and the United States of America, London, October 20, 1818.

" Whereas differences of opinion have arisen respecting the liberty claimed by the United States for the inhabitants thereof to take, dry, and cure fish on certain coasts, bays, harbours, and creeks of His Britannic Majesty's dominions in America, it is agreed between the high contracting parties that the inhabitants of the said United States shall have for ever, in common with the subjects of His Britannic Majesty, the liberty to take fish of every kind on that part of the coast of Newfoundland which extends from Cape Ray to the Rameau Islands, on the western and northern coast of Newfoundland from the said Cape Ray to the Quirpon Islands, on the shores of the Magdalen Islands, and also on the coasts, bays, harbours, and creeks from Mount Joly on the southern coast of Labrador to and through the Straits of Belleisle, and thence northwardly indefinitely along the coast, without prejudice, however, to any of the exclusive rights of the Hudson's Bay Company; and that the American fishermen shall also have liberty for ever to dry and cure fish on any of the unsettled bays, harbours, and creeks of the southern parts of the coast of Newfoundland and of the coast of Labrador; but as soon as the same or any portion thereof shall be settled, it shall not be lawful for the said fishermen to dry or cure fish without previous agreement for such purpose with the inhabitants, proprietors, or possessors of the ground. And the United States hereby renounce for ever any liberty heretofore enjoyed or claimed by the inhabitants thereof to take, dry, or cure fish on or within three marine miles of any of the coasts, bays, creeks, or harbours of His Britannic Majesty's dominion in America not included within the above-mentioned limits; provided, however, that the American fishermen shall be permitted to enter such bays or harbours for the purpose of shelter and of repairing damages therein, of purchasing wood, and of obtaining water, and for no other purpose whatever; but they shall be under such restrictions as may be necessary to prevent their taking, drying, or curing fish therein, or in any other manner abusing the privileges hereby reserved to them.

"It is agreed that a line, drawn from the most north-western point of the Lake of the Woods along the forty-ninth parallel of north latitude, or if the said point shall not be in the forty-ninth parallel of north latitude, then that a line drawn from the same point due north or south, as the case may be, until the said line shall intersect the said parallel, shall be the line of demarcation between the territories of the United States and those of His Britannic Majesty; and that the said line shall form the northern boundary of the said territories of the United States and the southern boundaries of the territories of His Britannic Majesty from the Lake of Woods to the Stony Mountains."

Agreement between Great Britain and the United States of America, June 5, 1884.

"It is agreed by the high contracting parties, that in addition to the liberty reserved to the United States fishermen by the above-mentioned Convention of October 20, 1818, of taking, curing, and drying fish on certain coasts of the British North American Colonies thereon defined, the inhabitants of the United States shall have, in common with the subjects of Her Britannic Majesty, the liberty to take fish of every kind, except shell-fish, on the sea-coasts and shores and in the bays, harbours, and creeks of Canada, New Brunswick, Nova Scotia, Prince Edward's Island, and of the several islands thereunto adjacent, without

being restricted to any distance from the shore; with
permission to land upon the coasts and shores of those
Colonies, and the islands thereof, and also upon the
Magdalen Islands, for the purpose of drying their nets
and curing their fish; provided that in so doing they
do not interfere with the rights of private property, or
with British fishermen in the peaceable use of any part
of the said coast in their occupancy for the same purpose.

"It is understood that the above-mentioned liberty
applies solely to the sea fishery, and that the salmon
and shad fisheries, and all fisheries in rivers and the
mouths of rivers, are herely reserved for British
fishermen.

Art. II. It is agreed by the high contracting
parties that British subjects shall have, in common
with the citizens of the United States, the liberty to
take fish of every kind, except shell-fish, on the
eastern sea-coasts and shores of the United States north
of the thirty-sixth parallel of north latitude, and on
the shores of the several islands thereunto adjacent,
and in the bays, harbours, and creeks of the said sea-
coasts and shores of the United States and of the said
islands, without being restricted to any distance from
the shore; with permission to land upon the said
coasts of the United States and of the islands aforesaid for the purpose of drying their nets and curing
their fish; provided that in so doing they do not interfere with the rights of private property, or with the
fishermen of the United States in the peaceable use of

any part of the said coasts in their occupancy for the same purpose. It is understood that the above-mentioned liberty applies solely to the sea fishery, and that salmon and shad fisheries, and all fisheries in rivers and mouths of rivers, are hereby reserved exclusively for fishermen of the United States."

Differences having arisen as regards the extent of the renunciation made by the United States as expressed in the Convention of 1818, and several seizures of American vessels having been made in Canada, a Bill was passed in the United States on February 28, 1887, authorizing the President to protect and defend the rights of American fishing vessels, American fishermen, American trading and other vessels, in certain cases. But the difference has been adjusted by the appointment of a Fishery Commission, composed of three members from each side, with power to deal with all the questions affecting the North American Fisheries.

North Sea Fisheries.—Convention between Belgium, Denmark, France, Germany, Great Britain, and the Netherlands, for regulating the Police of the North Sea Fisheries, May 15, 1882.

"1. The provisions of the present Convention, the object of which is to regulate the police of the fisheries in the North Sea outside territorial waters, shall apply to the subjects of the high contracting parties.

" 2. The fishermen of each country shall enjoy the exclusive right of fishery within the distance of three miles from low-water mark along the whole extent of the coasts of their respective countries, as well as of their dependent islands and banks. As regards bays, the distance of three miles shall be measured from a straight line drawn across the bay, in the part nearest the entrance, at the first point where the width does not exceed ten miles.

" The present Article shall not in any way prejudice the freedom of navigation and anchorage in territorial waters accorded to fishing boats, provided they conform to the special police regulations enacted by the Powers to whom the shores belong.

" 3. The miles mentioned in the preceding Article are geographical miles, whereof sixty make a degree of latitude."

Art. 4 fixes the limits of the North Sea.

See also the following Treaties :—

Newfoundland, Great Britain, and France, January 14, 1857.
Russia and Sweden, April 6, 1872.
Baden and Switzerland, March 25, 1875.
Austria and Italy, November 24, 1875.
Italy and Switzerland, November 8, 1882.
Belgium and Netherlands, September 3, 1884.

220. THE status of slavery is abolished in all civilized States.

Bologna in 1256 enfranchised all the slaves. In 1289 slavery was abolished in Florence.

A decision of the Courts in England in 1772, in the case of the negro (*Somerset* v. *Stewart*, Lofft 1), declared that as soon as a slave set his foot on English soil he became free. Cooper, writing in 1784, in his "Task" says, "Slaves cannot breathe in England; if their lungs receive our air, that moment they are free; they touch our country and their shackles fall." This sentiment re-echoed that of an earlier writer relating to France: "Servi peregrini, ut primum Galliæ fines penetraverint eodem momento liberi siunt" (Boedinus, lib. i. c. 5).

221. The slave-trade is illegal, and those who deal in slaves commit a crime.

In 1787 a society was formed in London for the suppression of the slave-trade; an Order in Council in 1805 prohibited the slave-trade in the British West Indies; and on March 25, 1807, an Act was passed making all slave-trade illegal after January 1, 1808. By Treaties concluded with Portugal on February 19, 1810, and with Denmark on January 14, 1814, stipulations were made in favour of the abolition of the slave-trade. And by the Treaty of Paris of May 30, 1814, it was provided that France should unite with England in obtaining, at a future Congress, from all Christian Powers the abolition of the slave-trade. The Congress of Vienna of 1815, of Aix-la-Chapelle of 1818, of Verona in 1822, adopted the same principle. But notwithstanding these special Treaties between the different Powers, the abolition of the slave-trade was not held as a principle of international Law. In 1841 a Treaty was concluded between Great Britain, Austria, France, Prussia, and Russia, which not only declared the slave-trade illegal, but gave to the contracting Powers a right of searching merchant vessels suspected of being engaged in the same. France, however, refused to ratify the Treaty, and the other Powers ratified it on February 19, 1842. Since then the leading Powers have given their concurrence to this principle, and have entered into obligations to co-operate in preventing the slave-trade. The principal clauses of the Treaties are as follows :—

[*Treaty clauses between Great Britain, Austria, Prussia, and Russia, signed at London, December 20, 1851 ; France, May 29, 1845 ; Belgium, February 24, 1848 ; the Netherlands, May 4, 1818, and August 31, 1848 ; the United States, February 17, 1862, and June*

3, 1870; *Portugal, July* 3, 1842, *and July* 18, 1871; *Egypt, August* 4, 1877; *Germany, March* 29, 1879; *Turkey, January* 25, 1883.]

222. The Treaty Powers engage to prohibit all trade in slaves, either by their respective subjects or under their respective flags, or by means of capital belonging to their respective subjects, and to declare such traffic piracy. Also that any vessel which may attempt to carry on the slave-trade shall by that fact alone lose all right to the protection of their flag.

223. The contracting parties consent that ships of war may be provided with power to search every merchant vessel belonging to any one of the contracting parties which shall, on reasonable grounds, be suspected of being engaged in the traffic in slaves, or of having been fitted out for that purpose, or of having been engaged in the traffic during the voyage in which she shall have been met with by the said cruisers, and that such cruisers may detain and send or carry away such vessels, in order that they may be sent to trial; the said essential right of search not to be exercised within the Mediterranean Sea.

224. Each of the contracting parties may choose to employ cruisers for the suppression of the slave-trade, notification being sent of the fact to the other parties.

225. Wherever a merchant vessel sailing under the flag of one of the contracting parties shall have been detained by a cruiser of the other, duly authorized to that effect, such merchant vessel, the master, the crew, the cargo, and the slaves who may be on board shall be brought into such place as the contracting parties shall have respectively designated for that purpose, and they shall be delivered over to the authorities appointed with that view by the Government within whose possessions such place is situated, in order that proceedings may be had with respect to them before the competent tribunals.

226. Proceedings shall be immediately taken against the vessel detained, her master, her crew, and her cargo, before the competent tribunal of the country to which she belongs, and they shall be tried and adjudged according to the established forms and laws in force in that country; and if it results from the proceedings that the said vessel was employed in the slave-trade, or

fitted out for that traffic, the vessel, her fittings, and her cargo of merchandise shall be confiscated, and the master, the crew, and their accomplices shall be dealt with conformably to the laws by which they shall have been tried.

227. In case of confiscation the proceeds of the sale of the aforesaid vessel shall, within the space of six months, reckoning from the date of the sale, be placed at the disposal of the Government of the country to which the ship which made the capture belongs, in order to be employed in conformity with the laws of that country.

228. By the Treaty between Her Majesty and the King of Portugal of July 3, 1842, and July 18, 1821, Portugal agreed to unite in the same effort.

229. By a Convention between France and Great Britain, dated London, May 29, 1845, France entered into the same obligations.

230. By a Treaty between Great Britain, Austria, Prussia, and Russia on the one part, and Belgium on the other, dated London, February 24, 1848, Belgium acceded to the Treaty of December 20 1841.

231. On August 31, 1848, several Articles were added to the Treaty of May 4, 1818, signed at the Hague, between Great Britain and the Netherlands, extending the boundary and removing the limits to the number of ships employed in the suppression of the slave-trade.

232. By a Treaty between Her Majesty and the United States of America, signed April 7, 1862, amended by the Treaties of February 17, 1863, and June 3, 1870, the United States joined in exercising the right of search and the institution of mixed courts of justice to decide all cases of capture.

233. By a Convention between the British and Egyptian Governments of August 4, 1877, the Egyptian Government engaged to prohibit absolutely the importation of slaves and to punish any person found engaged in the traffic in slaves ; also to pursue as murderers all persons who may be found engaged in the mutilation of or traffic in children.

234. By a Convention between the Government of Great Britain and the German Empire of March 29, 1879, the provisions of the Treaty

of December 20, 1841, were extended to the German Empire.

235. By a Convention between Her Majesty the Queen of Great Britain and Ireland and His Majesty the Sultan of January 25, 1880, and a declaration signed March 3, 1883, Turkey reserved absolutely the prohibition of the slave-trade, engaged to forbid the importation of slaves, and to pursue as criminals all persons who may be found engaged in the mutilation of or traffic in children.

236. Treaties regarding the slave-trade also exist with Abyssinia, the Argentine Confederation, Bolivia, Chile, Equator, Mexico, New Grenada, Persia, Texas, Uruguay, and Zanzibar.

237. Engagements have also been obtained from the following African Chiefs to prohibit the import or export of slaves, to close the public markets for slaves, and to protect all liberated slaves :—

> Sultan of Zanzibar, June 5, 1873.
> Nukeeb of Maculla, April 7, 1873.
> Sultan of Johanna, March 8, 1873, October 10, 1882.
> Sultan of Muscat, April 14, 1873.
> Jemadar of Shuhr, November 17, 1873.
> King of Dahomey, May 12, 1877.
> Sultan of Mohilla, October 24, 1882.
> King of Abyssinia, June 3, 1884.

CHAPTER XIV.

POSTAL COMMUNICATION.

SECTION I.—UNIVERSAL POSTAL UNION.

A TREATY for the formation of a General Postal Union was signed at Berne on October 9, 1874, between Austria-Hungary, Belgium, Denmark, Egypt, France, Germany, Great Britain, Greece, Italy, Luxembourg, Netherlands, Norway, Portugal, Roumania, Russia, Servia, Spain, Sweden, Switzerland, Turkey, and the United States. This Treaty was revised by the Convention of Paris of June, 1878, between the countries already named and the following :—The Argentine Republic, Brazil, certain British Colonies, the Danish Colonies, the French Colonies, Japan, Mexico, Montenegro, the Netherlands Colonies, Persia, Peru, the Portuguese Colonies, and Salvador. A new Convention was signed at Lisbon on November 3, 1880, with provisions for the Parcel Post. And by a Convention signed at Lisbon on March 21, 1885, several modifications were made in the previous Conventions, and the following additional countries became parties to the same, viz. Bolivia, Bulgaria, Chile, the United States of Colombia, Costa Rica, Dominica, Guatemala, Hayti, Hawai, Liberia, Nicaragua, Paraguay, Siam, Uruguay, and Venezuela.

The principal clauses of such Treaties are as follow :—

238. The countries between which the present Convention is concluded, as well as those which may join it hereafter, form, under the title of " Universal Postal Union," a single postal terri- tory for the reciprocal exchange of correspondence between their Post-offices.

239. The stipulations of this Convention extend to letters, post-cards, printed papers of every kind, commercial papers, and patterns or samples of merchandise, originating in one of the countries of the Union and intended for another of those countries. They also apply, as far as regards conveyance within the Union, to the exchange by post of the articles above mentioned between the Countries of the Union and countries foreign to the Union whenever that exchange makes use of the services of two of the con- tracting parties at least.

240. The right of transit is guaranteed throughout the entire territory of the Union.

241. There is maintained, under the name of the " International Bureau of the Universal Postal Union," a central Office, which is conducted under the surveillance of the Swiss Postal Administration, and the expenses of which are borne by all the offices of the Union.

242. In case of disagreement between two or more members of the Union as to the interpretation of the present Treaty, the question in dispute shall be decided by arbitration. To that end each of the offices concerned shall choose another member of the Union not interested in the affair. The decision of the arbitrators shall be given by an absolute majority of votes. In case of an equality of votes, the arbitrators shall choose, with the view of settling the difference, another Administration equally uninterested in the question in dispute.

To the Treaty are appended detailed regulations for the execution of the Treaty concluded at Berne.

243. Congresses of plenipotentiaries of the

countries participating in the Convention, or
simple administrative conferences, according to
the importance of the question to be solved, are
held, when a demand for them is made or approved by two-thirds at least of the Governments
or administrations, as the case may be. But a
Congress shall be held at least once every five
years.

SECTION II.—INTERNATIONAL CONVENTION FOR THE PROTECTION OF SUBMARINE TELEGRAPH CABLES.

*[Convention between the Argentine Confederation,
Austria-Hungary, Belgium, Brazil, Costa Rica, Den-
mark, Dominican Republic, France, Germany, Great
Britain and Ireland, Greece, Guatemala, Italy, Luxem-
bourg, Netherlands, Persia, Portugal, Roumania,
Russia, Salvador, Servia, Spain, Sweden and Norway,
Turkey, the United States of America, United States
of Colombia, and Uruguay (Paris, March 14, 1874).]*

244. The Convention applies outside territorial waters to all legally established submarine
cables, landed on the territories or possessions of
one or more of the high contracting parties.

245. It is a punishable offence to break or
injure a submarine cable, wilfully and by culpable

negligence, in such manner as might interrupt
or obstruct telegraphic communication, either
wholly or partially, such punishment being without prejudice to any civil action for damages.
This provision does not apply to cases where
those who break or injure a cable do so with the
lawful object of saving their lives or their ships,
after they have taken every necessary precaution
to avoid so breaking or injuring the cable.

246. The contracting parties undertake that,
on granting a concession for landing a submarine
cable, they will insist, so far as possible, upon
proper measures of safety being taken, both as
regards the track of the cable and its dimensions.

247. It is understood that the stipulations
of the present Convention do not in any way
restrict the freedom of action of belligerents.

Section III.—International Telegraphs.

[*Convention between Austria-Hungary, Belgium,
Denmark, France, Germany, Greece, Italy, Netherlands, Persia, Portugal, Russia, Spain, Sweden and
Norway, Switzerland, and Turkey, to guarantee and
to facilitate the International Telegraph Service. To*

this Treaty Great Britain acceded on December 21, 1875 (*St. Petersburg,* 1875).]

248. The contracting parties recognize the right of all persons to correspond by means of the international telegraphs.

249. They undertake to adopt all accessary measures to secure the secrecy of messages and their prompt despatch.

250. They, however, announce that they accept no responsibility on account of the service of the international telegraphs.

251. Each Government undertakes to devote to the international telegraph service, special wires, in sufficient number to ensure the rapid transmission of telegrams. These wires shall be established and worked in the best manner that experience in the service has made known.

252. Government and service telegrams may be forwarded on all occasions in secret language. Private telegrams in secret language may be exchanged between two States which admit that mode of correspondence. States which do not admit private telegrams in secret language to

emanate from, or terminate at, their offices, will allow them to pass in transit, unless the service be suspended.

253. The contracting parties reserve to themselves the power to stop the transmission of any private telegram which may appear dangerous to the security of the State, or which may be contrary to the laws of the country, to public order, or decency.

254. Each Government also reserves to itself the power to interrupt the system of the international telegraphs for an indefinite period, if it judges it necessary, either generally or only upon certain lines and for certain kinds of messages, upon condition that it immediately advises each of the other contracting Governments.

255. A central office, placed under the superior authority of the chief administration of one of the contracting Governments designated for that purpose in the service regulations, is appointed to collect, arrange, and publish information of all kinds relating to international telegraphy.

256. Administrative conferences will take

place periodically ; such conference fixing the
time and place of the next meeting.

SECTION IV.—MONEY ORDERS.

*[Conventions also exist relating to Money Orders
between Great Britain and Belgium, September 26,
1871, and January 1, 1882; Great Britain and Denmark, April 22, 1871, and January 26, 1882; Japan,
May 10, 1881; Portugal, January 17, 1883; Austria-
Hungary, June 3, 1883; France and Canada, June 20,
1884; Italy, March 4, 1872, and November 5, 1881;
Sweden, September 7, 1881.]*

257. The remittance of sums of money may
be made by means of post-office orders.

258. The post-offices of the contracting
parties are authorized to determine by common
agreement, and to modify, when required, the
measures necessary for the execution of the
Convention.

259. Each Power has also the right to
regulate the rate of commission on the issue of
the money orders which shall be delivered by its
officers. It is, however, agreed that the rate in
question shall not exceed two per cent.

Section V.—Immunities of Mail Packets.

By a Convention between the United Kingdom and France relative to communication by post, dated September 24, 1856, it was agreed as follows:—

Art. V. When the packets employed by the British Post Office, or by the French Post Office, in execution of Art. I. and II. of the present Convention, are national vessels, the property of Government, or vessels chartered or subsidized by Government, they shall be considered and treated as vessels of war in the ports of the two countries at which they regularly or accidentally touch, and be there entitled to the same honours and privileges. These packets shall be exempted in the said ports, as well upon their entrance as upon their departure, from all tonnage, navigation, and port dues, excepting however the vessels freighted or subsidized by Government, which must pay such dues in those ports where they are levied on behalf of corporations, private companies, or individuals. They shall not on any account be diverted from their especial duty, or be liable to seizure, detention, embargo, or *arrêt de Prince*.

Art. VI. The packets of the two Offices shall be at liberty to take on board, or land at the ports of the two countries at which they touch, whether regularly or accidentally, specie and gold and silver bullion, as well as passengers of whatever nation they may be, with their wearing apparels or luggage, on condition that the captains of these packets shall submit to the sanitary, police, and customs regulations of these ports concerning the arrival and departure of travellers. Nevertheless, the passengers admitted on board these packets who do not think fit to land during the stay at one of the said ports, shall not under any pretext be removed from on board, be liable to any search, or be subjected to the formality of a *visa* of their passports.

Art. XI. In case of war between the two nations, the packets of the two Offices shall continue their navigation until a notification is made on the part of either of the two Governments of the discontinuance of the postal communications, in which case they shall be permitted to return freely and under special protection to their respective ports.

CHAPTER XV.

MONETARY UNION.

260. WITH a view to establish more complete harmony between their monetary legislation, and to remedy the inconvenience which resulted to the people of their respective States from the diversity of titles in their silver token coins, France, Belgium, Italy, and Switzerland (the so-called Latin Union) entered into a Convention, dated December 23, 1865, under which the gold and silver standard coins of each country were made current throughout the territories of the Union, and circulation was also given to the silver token coins of the several States to an amount not exceeding six francs per head of the population of each. In 1868 Greece joined the Union. The Treaty was for fifteen years, and in anticipation of the end of that period, on

November 5, 1878, a fresh Convention was signed, prolonging the Union for a further period of six years from January 1, 1880, and introducing some modifications into the terms of the agreement. In 1884 the Monetary Convention was denounced by all the contracting States. But on November 6, 1885, the Convention was renewed for a further period of five years from January 1, 1886.

CHAPTER XVI.

INDUSTRIAL PROPERTY

SECTION I.—PATENT LAWS.

See the Patents, Designs, and Trade Marks Act, 1883, for the United Kingdom ; the Patent Laws of France of July 5, 1884, Germany, July 1, 1877, Italy, January 31, 1864, and of the United States, June 22, 1874.

261. The Patent Law of any State has no force as such in any other State.

262. A patent is a protection extended by the State to any of its own subjects for their exclusive use for a definite time, and on certain conditions, of any useful invention or designs.

263. A patent is granted for a new manufacture, including an improvement in or addition to a manufacture, a machine, or instrument, or

chemical discovery, or anything which is sub-
stantial and new.

264. A patent may be also granted to the pro-
prietor of any new or original design, the same
being duly registered.

In the United Kingdom any person, whether a
British subject or not, may make an application for
a patent. In France a foreigner may obtain a patent
of invention. In the United Kingdom an application
must contain a declaration to the effect that the
applicant is in possession of an invention, whereof
he or, in the case of a joint application, one or more
of the applicants claims or claim to be the true
and first inventor or inventors, and for which he or
they desires or desire to obtain a patent; and must
be accompanied by either a provisional or complete
specification. In the United Kingdom an invention
means any manner of new manufacture. In France
a patent is granted for every new discovery or invention in all departments of industry, for any new
industrial product, new method, or new application of
known methods for obtaining industrial results. In
Germany a patent is granted for any new invention which can be turned to account in trade. In
Italy an invention or discovery is said to belong to
industry whenever its immediate product or result re-
lates to industrial pursuits. Any instrument, machine,

tool, engine, or any mechanical arrangement ; a process or method of manufacture ; a motor or the application of any known power to industrial purposes ; and also the technical application of a scientific principle, can be the subject of a patent, provided immediate results in industry are obtained thereby. In the United States a patent is granted to any person who has invented or discovered any new and useful art, machine, manufacture, or composition of matter, or any new and useful improvement thereof not known or used by others in the country.

265. A trade mark is any distinctive device, mark, brand, heading, label, ticket, or fancy words, or even a name of an individual, or form printed, impressed, or woven in some particular and distinct manner intended to mark or distinguish the goods or production of any distinct person.

266. A trade mark may be registered for particular goods or classes of goods.

267. A trade mark, when registered, may be assigned and transmitted only in connection with the good-will of the business concerned in the particular goods or classes of goods for which it has been registered, and shall be determinable with that good-will.

268. By the British law it is provided that if Her Majesty should make any arrangement with the Government of any foreign State for mutual protection of inventions, designs, and trade marks, or any of them, then any person who has applied for protection for any invention, design, or trade mark in any such State shall be entitled to a patent for his invention, or to registration of his design or trade mark, as the case may be, in priority to other applicants; and such patent or registration shall have the same date as the date of the protection obtained in such foreign State, provided that his application is made, in the case of a patent, within seven months, and in the case of a design or trade mark, within four months, from his applying for protection in the foreign State with which the arrangement is in force.

SECTION II.—TREATY CLAUSES CONCERNING INDUSTRIAL PROPERTY.

[International Convention between Belgium, Brazil, France, Guatemala, Italy, Netherlands, Portugal, Salvador, Spain, Servia, and Switzerland, signed at **Paris, March 20, 1883.** *Ratification exchanged at*

Paris, June 6, 1884. On April 2, 1884, Great Britain and Ireland acceded to the Convention (Paris, March 20, 1883).]

269. The subjects or citizens of each of the contracting States shall in all the other States of the Union, as regards patents, industrial designs or models, trade marks, and trade names, enjoy the advantages that their respective laws now grant or shall hereafter grant to their own subjects or citizens.

270. Consequently they shall have the same protection as the latter, and the same remedy against any infringement of their rights, provided they observe the formalities and conditions imposed on subjects or citizens by the internal legislation of each State.

271. Subjects or citizens of States, not forming part of the Union, who are domiciled or have industrial or commercial establishments in the territory of any of the States of the Union, shall be assimilated to the subjects or citizens of the contracting States.

272. Any person who has duly applied for a patent, industrial design or model, or trade

mark in one of the contracting States shall enjoy, as regards registration in the other States, and reserving the rights of third parties, a right of priority during the periods hereinafter stated.

273. Consequently, subsequent registration in any of the other States of the Union before expiry of those periods shall not be invalidated through any acts accomplished in the interval, either, for instance, by another registration, by publication of the invention, or by the working of it by a third party, by the sale of copies of the design or model, or by use of the trade mark.

274. The above-mentioned terms of priority shall be six months for patents, and three months for industrial designs, and models, and trade marks. A month longer is allowed for countries beyond sea.

275. The introduction by the patentee into the country where the patent has been granted of objects manufactured in any of the States of the Union shall not entail forfeiture. Nevertheless, the patentee shall remain bound to work his patent in conformity with the laws of the country into which he introduces his patented objects.

276. Every trade mark duly registered in the country of origin shall be admitted for registration and protected in the form originally registered in all the other countries of the Union.

277. That country shall be deemed the country of origin where the applicant has his chief seat of business.

278. If the chief seat of business is not situated in one of the countries of the Union, the country to which the applicant belongs shall be deemed the country of origin. Registration may be refused if the object for which it is solicited is considered contrary to morality or public order.

279. The nature of the goods on which the trade mark is to be used can in no case be an obstacle to the registration of the trade mark.

280. A trade name shall be protected in all the countries of the Union without necessity of registration, whether it forms part or not of a trade mark.

281. All goods illegally bearing a trade mark or trade name may be seized on importation into

those States of the Union where that mark or name has a right to legal protection.

282. The seizure shall be effected at the request of either the proper public department, or of the interested party pursuant to the internal legislation of such country.

283. The provisions of the preceding article shall apply to all goods falsely bearing the name of any locality as indication of the place of origin where such indication is associated with a trade name of a fictitious character, or assumed with a fraudulent intention.

284. Any manufacturer of or trader in such goods, established in the locality falsely designated as the place of origin, shall be deemed an interested party.

285. The contracting parties agree to grant temporary protection to patentable inventions, to industrial designs or models, or trade marks, for articles exhibited at official or officially recognized International Exhibitions.

286. Each of the contracting parties agree to establish a special Government department for

industrial property, and a central office for communication to the public of patents, industrial designs or models, and trade marks.

287. An international office shall be organized under the name of "Bureau International de l'Union pour la Protection de la Propriété Industrielle" (International Office of the Union for the Protection of Industrial Property).

288. This office, the expense of which shall be defrayed by the Governments of all the contracting States, shall be placed under the high authority of the central administration of the Swiss Confederation, and shall work under its supervision.   Its functions shall be determined by agreement between the States of the Union.

289. The present Convention shall be submitted to periodical revisions, with a view to introducing improvements calculated to perfect the system of the Union.

290. To this end conferences shall be successively held in one of the contracting States by delegates.

291. It is agreed that the contracting parties

respectively reserve to themselves the right to make separately, as between themselves, special arrangements for the protection of industrial property, in so far as such arrangements do not contravene the provisions of the present Convention.

292. States which have not taken part in the present Convention shall be permitted to adhere to it at their request.

Such adhesion shall be notified officially through the diplomatic channel to the Government of the Swiss Confederation, and by the latter to all the others. It shall imply complete accession to all the clauses, and admission to all the advantages stipulated by the present Convention.

293. The execution of the reciprocal engagements contained in the present Convention is subordinated, in so far as necessary, to the observance of the formalities and rules established by the constitutional laws of those of the contracting parties who are bound to procure the application of the same, which they engage to do with as little delay as possible.

294. The present Convention shall come into operation one month after the exchange of ratifications, and shall remain in force for an unlimited time, till the expiry of one year from the date of its denunciation. This denunciation shall be addressed to the Government commissioned to receive adhesions. It shall only affect the denouncing State, the Convention remaining in operation as regards the other contracting parties.

295. The present Convention shall be ratified, and the ratifications exchanged in Paris, within one year at the latest.

296. The subjects or citizens of each of the contracting parties shall have in the dominions and possessions of the other the same rights as belong to native subjects or citizens, or as are now granted, or may hereafter be granted, to the subjects or citizens of the most favoured nation, in everything relating to property in trade marks and trade labels.

297. It is understood that any person who desires to obtain the aforesaid protection must fulfil the formalities required by the laws of the respective countries.

The Senate of the United States having ratified the Convention of March 20, 1883, for the protection of industrial property, as well as the Protocol adopted May 11, 1886, by the Conference of Rome, the Government of the United States have acceded to the Union from May 30, 1887, the date of the notification addressed by the United States Government to the Swiss Legation, and the United States will rank in the first class as far as regards their participation in the expenses of the International Office. The adhesion, however, is under the reserve that, inasmuch as the right of legislating respecting manufacturing or commercial marks is, to a certain degree, reserved to each of the States of the American Union, the stipulations of the Convention shall only be applicable within the limits of the constitutional powers of the high contracting parties.

The following Treaties on Trade Marks have been concluded :—

EUROPEAN STATES.

Austria-Hungary.

United States, November 25, 1871; Russia, February 5, 1874; Belgium, January 12, 1880.

Belgium.

Saxony, March 11, 1866; Italy, May 28, 1872; Germany, September 10, 1875; Denmark, November 15, 1875; Brazil, September 2, 1876; Austria, January 12, 1880; Netherlands, October 22, 1880; Russia, January 29, 1881; Switzerland, February 11, 1881; Roumania, March 8, 1881; Venezuela, May

25, 1882; Luxembourg, September 25, 1883; United States, April 7, 1886.

Denmark.

Belgium, November 15, 1875; Great Britain, November 15, 1879; France, April 7, 1880; Netherlands, January 14, 1881.

France.

Italy, June 10, 1874; Brazil, April 12, 1876; Spain, June 30, 1876; Venezuela, May 3, 1879; Luxembourg, March 27, 1880; Denmark, April 7, 1880; Switzerland, February 23, 1882.

Germany.

Saxony with Belgium, March 11, 1866; Russia, January 20, 1873; Belgium, September 10, 1875; Netherlands, December 28, 1881.

Great Britain.

Borneo, May 27, 1847, August 17, 1878; Russia, July 11, 1871; Spain, December 14, 1875; Denmark, November 15, 1879; Portugal, January 20, 1880; Switzerland, November 6, 1880.

Italy.

Brazil, July 21, 1877; Belgium, May 28, 1872; France, June 10, 1874; United States, June 1, 1882.

Luxembourg.

Belgium, September 25, 1883.

Netherlands.

Brazil, July 26, 1878; Luxembourg and France, May 27, 1880; Belgium, October 22, 1880; Denmark, January 14, 1881; Russia, April 7, 1881; Switzerland, May 27, 1881; Germany, December 28, 1881.

Portugal.

Great Britain, January 20, 1880.

Roumania.

Belgium, March 8, 1881.

Russia.

Great Britain, July 11, 1871; Russia, January 23, 1873; Austria, February 5, 1874; Belgium, January 29, 1881.

Spain.

France, June 30, 1876; Great Britain, December 14, 1885; United States, June 19, 1882.

Switzerland.

Great Britain, November 6, 1880; Belgium, February 11, 1881; Netherlands, December 28, 1881; France, February 23, 1882.

AMERICAN STATES.

Brazil.

France, April 12, 1876; Belgium, September 2, 1876; Italy, July 21, 1877; Netherlands, July 26, 1878; United States, September 24, 1878.

United States.

Russia, January 26, 1868, March 28, 1874; Austria-Hungary, November 25, 1871; Great Britain, October 24, 1877; Brazil, September 24, 1878; Italy, June 1, 1882; Spain, June 19, 1882; Belgium, April 7, 1886.

Venezuela.

France, May 3, 1879; Belgium, May 25, 1882.

Borneo

Great Britain, May 27, 1847.

CHAPTER XVII.

COPYRIGHT.

SECTION I.—COPYRIGHT LAWS.

298. COPYRIGHT is the exclusive right of an author to copy, print, engrave, photograph, translate, abridge, or multiply what he has himself produced by pen, pencil, or chisel.

299. The object of copyright is to increase the general stock of learning within the country, and to protect the author, thereby inducing him to publish his work.

In the United Kingdom copyright for books is for forty-two years from publication, or for the life of the author and a term of seven years from his death. In France copyright is guaranteed to authors and their widows during their lives, to their children for twenty years, and if they leave no children, to their heirs for ten years. In Prussia copyright continues for the author's life, and for thirty years after his death. In Austria the term is the same. In Holland copyright is limited to the life of the author and twenty years thereafter; in Denmark, it is for the author's life and thirty years; in Sweden, for life and twenty years; in Spain, for life and fifty years after; in Russia, for life and twenty-five years, and for ten years more if an edition is published within five years of the end of the first term. In Greece copyright is for fifteen years from publication; in Italy, for life and forty years, with a second term of forty years, during which any one can publish the work upon paying a royalty to the author or his assigns; in the United States, for twenty-eight years from the time of recording the title thereof, and for fourteen years more if recorded anew within six months before the expiration of the same.

300. The persons capable of obtaining copyright in any country are—(1) a natural born, or a naturalized subject, in which case the place of residence at the time of the publication of the book is immaterial; (2) a person who, at the time of the publication of the book in which copyright is to be obtained, owes local or temporary allegiance to the State, by residing at that time in some part of the same; and (3) an alien friend who first publishes a book in the

country, even although resident out of the same.

301. By Treaty a mutuality of literary protection has been secured, whereby the republication or piracy, in either country, of any work of literature or of art published in the other, shall be dealt with in the same manner as the republication or piracy of a work of the same nature first published in such other country.

SECTION II.—TREATY CLAUSES CONCERNING LITERATURE AND ART.

[Convention concerning the protection of literary and artistic works between France, Germany, Great Britain, Hayti, Honduras, Italy, the Netherlands, Spain, Sweden and Norway, Switzerland, and Tunis, September 18, 1885.] A conference was held at Berne, on September 6, 1886, for the purpose of signing the International Copyright Convention. But the Convention has not yet been laid before the British Parliament.

302. The contracting States are formed into a Union for the protection of the rights of authors over their literary and artistic works.

303. Authors of any of the countries of the Union, or their lawful representatives, are to enjoy in the other countries for their works, whether published in one of their countries or unpublished, the rights which the respective laws do now or may hereafter grant to natives.

304. The enjoyment of these rights in respect to the accomplishment of the conditions and formalities prescribed by law in the country of origin of the work, cannot exceed in the other countries the term of protection granted in the said country of origin.

305. The country of origin of the works is that in which the work is first published, or if such publication takes place simultaneously in several countries of the Union, that one of them in which the shortest term of protection is granted by law.

306. For unpublished works the country to which the author belongs is considered the country of origin of the work.

307. The stipulations of the present Convention apply equally to the publishers of literary

and artistic works published in one of the countries of the Union, but of which the authors belong to a country which is not a party to the Union.

308. The expression "literary and artistic works" comprehends books, pamphlets, and all other writings; dramatic or dramatico-musical works; musical compositions with or without words; works of design, painting, sculpture, and engraving; lithographs, illustrations, geographical charts; plans, sketches, and plastic works relative to geography, topography, architecture, or science in general; in fact, every production whatsoever in the literary, scientific, or artistic domain which can be published by any mode of impression or reproduction.

309. Authors of any of the countries of the Union, or their lawful representatives, shall enjoy in the other countries the exclusive right of making or authorizing the translation of their works until the expiration of ten years from the publication of the original work in one of the countries of the Union.

310. For works published in incomplete parts

(*livraisons*) the period of ten years commences from the date of publication of the last part of the original work.

311. For works composed of several volumes published at intervals, as well as for the bulletins or collections (*cahiers*) published by literary or scientific societies, or by private persons, each volume, bulletin, or collection is, with regard to the period of ten years, considered as a separate work.

312. In the cases provided for in the present article, and for the calculation of the period of protection, December 31 of the year in which the work was published is admitted as the date of publication.

313. Authorized translations are protected as original works. They consequently enjoy the protection stipulated in Arts. II. and III., as regards their unauthorized reproduction in the countries of the Union.

314. It is understood that, in the case of a work for which the translating right has fallen into the public domain, the translator cannot

oppose the translation of the same work by other writers.

315. Articles from newspapers or periodicals published in any of the countries of the Union may be reproduced in original or in translation in the other countries of the Union, unless the authors or publishers have expressly forbidden it. For periodicals it is sufficient if the prohibition is made in a general manner at the beginning of each number of the periodical.

316. This prohibition cannot in any case apply to articles of political discussion, or to the reproduction of news of the day *or current topics.*

317. As regards the liberty of extracting portions from literary or artistic works, for use in publications destined for educational or scientific purposes, or for chrestomathies, the matter is to be decided by the legislation of the different countries of the Union, or by special arrangements existing or to be concluded between them.

318. The stipulations of Art. II. apply to

the public representation of dramatic or dramatico-musical works, whether such works be published or not.

319. Authors of dramatic or dramatico-
musical works, or their lawful representatives,
are, during the existence of their exclusive right
of translation, equally protected against the
unauthorized public representation of translations
of their works.

320. The stipulations of Art. II. apply
equally to the public performance of unpublished
musical works, or of published works in which
the author has expressly declared on the title-
page or commencement of the work that he
forbids the public performance.

321. Unauthorized indirect appropriations of
a literary or artistic work, of various kinds, such
as *adaptations, arrangements of music, etc.*, are
specially included amongst the illicit reproduc-
tions to which the present Convention applies,
when they are only the reproduction of a
particular work in the same form, or in another
form with non-essential alterations, additions, or

11

abridgments, so made as not to confer the character of a new original work.

322. It is agreed that, in the application of the present article, the tribunals of the various countries of the Union will, if there is occasion, conform themselves to the provisions of their respective laws.

323. In order that the authors of works protected by the present Convention shall, in the absence of proof to the contrary, be considered as such, and be consequently admitted to institute proceedings against pirates before the courts of the various countries of the Union, it will be sufficient that their name be indicated on the work in the accustomed manner.

324. For anonymous or pseudonymous works, the publisher whose name is indicated on the work is entitled to protect the rights belonging to the author. He is, without other proof, reputed the lawful representative of the anonymous or pseudonymous author.

325. It is nevertheless agreed that the tribunals may, if necessary, require the production

of a certificate from the competent authority, to
the effect that the formalities prescribed by law
in the country of origin have been accomplished,
as contemplated in Art. II.

326. Pirated works may be seized on importation into those countries of the Union where
the original work enjoys legal protection.

The seizure shall take place conformably to
the domestic law of each State.

327. It is understood that the provisions of the
present Convention cannot in any way derogate
from the right belonging to the Government of
each country of the Union to permit, to control,
or to prohibit, by measures of domestic legislation or police, the circulation, representation, or
exhibition of any works or productions in regard
to which the competent authority may find it
necessary to exercise that right.

328. Under the reserves and conditions to be
determined by common agreement, the present
Convention applies to all works which, at the
moment of its coming into force, have not yet
fallen into the public domain in the country of
origin.

329. It is understood that the Governments of the countries of the Union reserve to themselves respectively the right to enter into separate and particular arrangements between each other, provided always that such arrangements confer upon authors or their lawful representatives more extended rights than those granted by the Union, or embody other stipulations not contrary to the present Convention.

330. An International Office is established, under the name of "Office of the International Union for the Protection of Literary and Artistic Works."

331. This office, of which the expenses will be borne by the Administrations of all the countries of the Union, is placed under the high authority of the superior Administration of the Swiss Confederation, and works under its direction. The functions of this office are determined by common accord between the countries of the Union.

332. The present Convention may be submitted to revisions, in order to introduce therein

amendments calculated to perfect the system of the Union.

333. Questions of this kind, as well as those which are of interest to the Union in other respects, will be considered in conferences to be held successively in the countries of the Union by delegates of the said countries.

334. It is understood that no alteration in the present Convention shall be binding on the Union except by the unanimous consent of the countries composing it.

335. Countries which have not become parties to the present Convention, and which grant by their domestic law the protection of rights secured by this Convention, shall be admitted to accede thereto on request to that effect.

336. Such accession shall be notified in writing to the Government of the Swiss Confederation, who will communicate it to all the other countries of the Union.

337. Such accession shall imply full adhesion

to all the clauses and admission to all the advantages by the present Convention.

338. Countries acceding to the present Convention shall also have the right to accede thereto at any time for their Colonies or foreign possessions.

339. They may do this either by a general declaration comprehending all these Colonies or possessions within the accession, or by specially naming those comprised therein, or by simply indicating those which are excluded.

340. The present Convention shall be put in force three months after the exchange of the ratifications, and shall remain in effect for an indefinite period, until the termination of a year from the day on which it may have been denounced.

341. Such denunciation shall be made to the Government authorized to receive accessions, and shall only be effective as regards the country making it, the Convention remaining in full force and effect for the other countries of the Union.

342. The present Convention shall be ratified, and the ratifications exchanged at Berne, within the space of one year at the latest.

The following special Treaties have been concluded on the subject of literary property :—

EUROPEAN STATES.

Austria-Hungary.

Saxony, May 26, 1865; France, January 5, 1879.

Belgium.

Spain, April 30, 1859, January 17, 1880; Prussia, March 28, 1863; Portugal, October 11, 1866; France, February 7, 1874 September 29, 1879, May 27, 1881.

France.

Belgium, May 27, 1861; Austria-Hungary, January 5, 1879; Germany, April 19, 1883.

Germany.

Italy, May 12, 1869, June 20, 1884; Switzerland, May 13, 1869, May 23, 1881; France, April 19, 1883.

Great Britain.

Prussia, May 13, 1846, June 14, 1855; Hanover, August 4, 1847; France, October 27, 1851; Switzerland, October 30, 1858; Spain, August 11, 1880. ·

Hanover

Great Britain, August 4, 1847.

Italy.

Germany, May 12, 1869, June 20, 1884; Switzerland, January 28, 1879; Spain, June 28, 1880; Sweden and Norway, October 9, 1884.

Portugal.

Belgium, October 11, 1866.

Prussia.

Great Britain, May 13, 1846, June 14, 1855; Belgium, March 28, 1863.

Saxony.

Austria, May 26, 1865.

Spain.

Belgium, April 30, 1859, January 16, 1880; Italy, June 28, 1880; Great Britain, August 11, 1880.

Sweden and Norway

Italy, October 9, 1884.

Switzerland.

Great Britain, October 30, 1858; Germany, May 13, 1869, May 23, 1881; Italy, January 28, 1879.

CHAPTER XVIII.

343. ALIENS are entitled to have free access to the courts of justice of the country where they reside, and are at liberty to employ advocates and agents for the conduct of their suits.

344. If the alien permanently resides abroad or out of the jurisdiction of the court, the judge may stay the proceedings in the action till he gives security for costs.

In France a foreigner bringing a suit must give bail for costs and interest, except in matters of commerce and trade; except also when the foreigner possesses in France immovable property of sufficient value to cover such costs and interest, and where the foreigner is by treaty exempt from the necessity of finding bail.

345. A conflict of law exists as to the com-

petency of the tribunals to entertain suits between undomiciled foreigners, etc., for breach of
an obligation contracted in a foreign State.

In France the French courts hold themselves incompetent. In England *all* persons are entitled to
maintain a suit as plaintiffs.

346. Corporations or other artificial persons
have no existence beyond the jurisdiction of the
State by virtue of which they exist, and have no
capacity beyond that which is conferred by the
law of such State. By treaty, however, the
corporate rights of such societies to sue or be
sued may be recognized.

TREATY CLAUSES AS REGARD JOINT STOCK COMPANIES.

*See British Treaties with Belgium, November 13,
1862; France, April 30, 1862; Germany, March 27,
1874; Spain, January 29, 1883. Austria-Hungary
with Italy, January 24, 1876. Belgium with Greece,
April 2, 1871; Venezuela, May 25, 1882. Germany
with Belgium, November 26, 1873, and Italy, August
8, 1873. Greece with Italy, February 25, 1871.*

347. Joint stock companies and other asso-
ciations, commercial, industrial, and financial,
constituted in conformity with the laws in force

in either State, may exercise in the dominions of the other all their rights, including that of appearing before tribunals for the purpose of bringing an action, or of defending themselves, with the sole condition, in exercising such rights, of always conforming themselves to the laws and customs in force in the said dominions.

The French Law of May 30, 1857, said that foreign societies. cannot sue or be sued in France unless under the authority of the Chief of the State. The Belgian Law of 1873 provided that anonymous and other industrial societies, having their principal seats in foreign countries, may carry on their business in Belgium and sue in the Belgian courts; that every society whose principal establishment is in Belgium is subject to Belgian laws, though the deed constituting the same was made in a foreign country. In England any foreign corporation or other artificial or moral person may sue, provided the local law of the transaction authorizes it to act in a corporate or other artificial capacity.

348. The *lex loci* governs all criminal jurisdiction.

The State is not bound to punish a foreign subject residing in the country for a crime committed against the subject of another State out of its jurisdiction.

349. The State will not recognize or allow to be executed a foreign judgment which contains any provision or order contrary to public morals or public policy.

350. A foreign judgment may be impeached if the tribunal which pronounced it was incompetent or was not duly seized or possessed of the subject of its decision, or if the defendant had not been fairly heard according to the law of the State.

CHAPTER XIX.

*See Treaties of Austria-Hungary with France,
May 14, 1879; Belgium, June 19, 1880; Servia, May
6, 1881; Italy, February 9, 1883; Switzerland, February 8, 1884. Germany with Luxembourg, June 12,
1879; France, February 20, 1880. Italy with Switzerland, February 8, 1884. Spain with Italy, July 8,
1882.*

351. The subjects and citizens of the contracting parties shall reciprocally enjoy the same
benefit of judicial assistance as the natives themselves, by conforming themselves to the laws of
the country in which such assistance shall be
claimed.

352. In all cases a certificate of indigence
will be given to a foreigner who may demand

assistance by the authorities where he habitually resides. If he does not reside in the place where the demand is made, the certificate of indigence shall be approved and legalized by the Diplomatic Agent of the place where the certificate has to be given. When the foreigner does reside in the place where the demand is made, information may also be taken from the authorities of the State to which he belongs.

353. Austro-Hungarians admitted in France, and the French admitted in Austria-Hungary, will not be required to give any guarantee or deposit which, under any name whatever, might be exacted of foreigners pleading against natives by the law of the place where the suit is to be introduced.

(*Declaration of Austria-Hungary and France, May* 14, 1879.)

CHAPTER XX.

TREATY CLAUSES CONCERNING THE RECIPROCAL COM-
MUNICATION OF ACTS OF THE CIVIL STATUS AND
OF PENAL SENTENCES.

See Treaties of Austria-Hungary with Belgium, April 30, 1871, and Italy, April 25, 1873, and September 29, 1883; Belgium with France, August 25, 1876, Italy, July 17, 1876, Luxembourg, March 21, 1879, Monaco, November 25, 1876, Roumania, March 4, 1881, Spain, January 27, 1872, and Switzerland, February 2, 1882. Also France with Italy, January 13, 1875, and Luxembourg, January 13, 1875.

354. The contracting parties engage to send to one another at stated times, and without expense, copies, duly legalized, of the acts of birth, marriage, and death, drawn up in their territories, and concerning the subjects of the other States.

355. The transmission of the acts of death

will extend besides to persons who, having died in Belgium, were born or, according to information supplied by local authorities, had their domicile in Switzerland. It will be the same for acts of death of persons who, having died in Switzerland, were born or, according to information supplied, had their domicile in Belgium.

356. The officers of the Civil State in Belgium and in Switzerland will give each other notice by diplomatic means of the legitimation of illegitimate children inscribed in the act of marriage.

357. Every six months, the copies of the said acts drawn up for the preceding six months will be sent by the Belgian Government to the Swiss Consulate at Brussels, and by the Federal Swiss Council to the Belgian Legation at Berne.

358. The acts drawn up in Belgium in the Flemish language, and the acts drawn up in Switzerland in the German or Italian language, will be accompanied with a French translation, duly certified by a competent authority.

359. It is expressly understood that the delivery or acceptance of the copies of the said

acts will not prejudice the question of nation-ality.   The granting of acts of Civil State demanded by either side at the request of private parties not provided by a certificate of indigence will be subject to the payment of fees exigible in the two countries (*Declaration between Belgium and Switzerland, February* 2, 1882).

360. The Italian and Brazilian Governments bind themselves to communicate to one another, by diplomatic means and by means of translations, the penal sentences, of whatever nature, pro-nounced by the tribunals of one of the two countries against the subjects of the other (*Declaration of Brazil and Italy, June* 2, 1879).

CHAPTER XXI.

TREATY CLAUSES CONCERNING EXTRADITION.

361. On the requisition made in the name of either of the contracting parties by their respective Diplomatic Agents, either engages to deliver up to each other reciprocally any person who, being accused or convicted of any of the crimes hereinafter specified, committed within the jurisdiction of the requiring party, shall be found within the territories of the other party.

362. The crimes for which extradition is granted are as follows :—

1. Murder, including assassination, parricide, infanticide, poisoning, or attempt to murder.
2. Manslaughter.
3. Administering drugs, or using instruments

with intent to procure the miscarriage of women.

4. Rape.

5. Aggravated or indecent assault; carnal knowledge of a girl above the age of ten years and under the age of twelve years; indecent assault upon any female, or any attempt to have carnal knowledge of a girl under twelve years of age.

6. Kidnapping and false imprisonment; childstealing; abandoning, exposing, or unlawfully detaining children.

7. Abduction of minors.

8. Bigamy.

9. Wounding or inflicting grievous bodily harm, when such acts cause permanent disease or incapacity for personal labour, or the absolute loss or privation of a member or organ.

10. Arson.

11. Burglary or housebreaking; robbing with violence; larceny or embezzlement.

12. Fraud by banker, agent, factor, trustee, director, member, or public officer of any company, made criminal by any law for the time being in force.

13. Obtaining money, valuable security, or goods by false pretences; receiving any money, valuable security, or other property, knowing the same to have been feloniously stolen or unlawfully obtained, the quantity or value of which shall be greater in amount than £200 sterling.

14. (*a*.) Counterfeiting or altering money, or bringing into circulation counterfeited or altered money.

(*b*.) Forgery, or counterfeiting, or altering, or knowingly uttering what is forged, counterfeited, or altered.

(*c*.) Knowingly making without lawful authority any instrument, tool, or engine adapted and intended for the counterfeiting of coins of the realm

15. Crimes against the bankruptcy law.

16. Any malicious act done with intent to endanger persons in a railway train.

17. Malicious injury to property, if such offence be indictable and punishable with one year's imprisonment or more.

18. Crimes committed at sea—

(*a*.) Piracy by the law of nations.

    (*b.*) Sinking or destroying a vessel at sea, or attempting or conspiring to do so.

    (*c.*) Revolt or conspiring to revolt among two or more persons on board a ship on the high seas against the authority of the master.

    (*d.*) Assault on board a ship on the high seas, with intent to destroy life or to do grievous bodily harm.

19. Dealing in slaves in such a manner as to constitute an offence against the laws of both countries.

The extradition is also to take place for participation in any of the aforesaid crimes, as an accessory before or after the fact, provided such participation be punishable by the laws of both contracting parties.

363. The British Treaties with France, Spain, and other countries name among the crimes:

Threats by letter or otherwise with intent to extort.

Perjury or subornation of perjury.

Assaulting a magistrate or peace or public officer.

364. The British Treaty of extradition with France provides that the same shall apply to crimes and offences committed prior to the signing of the Treaty ; but that a person surrendered shall not be tried for any crime or offence committed in the other country before the extradition, other than the crime for which his surrender has been granted.

365. No accused or convicted person shall be surrendered, if the offence in respect of which his surrender is demanded shall be deemed by the party upon which it is made to be a political offence, or to be an act connected with such an offence, or if he prove to the satisfaction of the police magistrate, or of the Court before which he is brought on *habeas corpus,* or of the Secretary of State, that the requisition for his surrender has, in fact, been made with a view to try or to punish him for an offence of a political character.

366. No subject of either country shall be delivered up by the Government of the one to the Government of the other. Within the denomination of subjects are included naturalized citizens of the country and all foreigners who,

according to the laws of either, are assimilated to subjects.

367. The extradition is not to take place if the person claimed on the part of the Government of either party has already been tried and discharged, or punished, or is still under trial in either country for the crime for which his extradition is demanded.

368. The extradition is not to take place if, subsequent to the commission of the crime or the conviction thereof, exemption from prosecution or punishment has been acquired by lapse of time, according to the laws of the State applied to.

369. A fugitive criminal is not to be surrendered if the offence in respect of which his surrender is demanded is one of a political character, or if he prove that the requisition for his surrender has in fact been made with a view to try or to punish him for an offence of a political character.

370. A person surrendered can in no case be kept in prison, or be brought to trial in the State to which the surrender has been made, for

any other crime or on account of any other matters than those for which the extradition shall have taken place, until he has been restored, or has had the opportunity of returning, to the country from whence he was surrendered.

371. The requisition for extradition must be made through the Diplomatic Agent of the contracting parties respectively.

372. The requisition for the extradition of an accused person must be accompanied by a warrant of arrest issued by the competent authority of the State requiring the extradition, and by such evidence as, according to the laws of the place where the accused is found, would justify his arrest, if the crime had been committed there.

European States.

Austria-Hungary.

Belgium, March 18, 1853, December 13, 1872, January 12, 1881; United States, July 5, 1856; Italy, February 27, 1869, March 30, 1875, November 17, 1877; Montenegro, September 23, 1872; Great Britain, December 3, 1873; Greece, March 28, 1874; Russia, October 15, 1874; Netherlands, November 24, 1880; Servia, May 6, 1881; Luxembourg, February 11, 1882; Brazil, May 2, 1883.

Bavaria.

Russia, September 15, 1865.

Belgium.

Venezuela, March 13, 1844; Austria, March 18, 1853, December 13, 1872, January 12, 1881; Spain, June 17, 1870, January 28, 1876; Great Britain, July 31, 1872, May 20, 1876, July 23, 1877; Russia, August 4, 1872, July 29, 1881; Italy, February 3, 1873, January 15, 1875; Brazil, June 21, 1873, May 2, 1883; United States, March 19, 1874, June 13, 1882; Peru, August 14, 1874; France, August 15, 1874; Germany, December 24, 1874; Portugal, March 8, 1875, December 16, 1881; Denmark, March 25, 1876; Netherlands, January 16, 1877; Salvador, February 27, 1880; Servia, March 23, 1881; Mexico, May 12, 1881.

Denmark.

Great Britain, April 15, 1862, March 31, 1873; Italy, February 19, 1873; Belgium, March 25, 1876; France, March 28, 1877; Netherlands, July 28, 1877.

France.

United States, November 2, 1843, February 10, 1858; Portugal, July 13, 1854, December 30, 1877; Italy, May 12, 1870, July 16, 1873; Belgium, August 15, 1874; Peru, September 30, 1874; Luxembourg, September 12, 1875; Monaco, July 8, 1876; Great Britain, August 14, 1876; Denmark, March 28, 1877.

Germany.

Prussia and Great Britain, March 5, 1864; Italy, July 25, 1873; Switzerland, January 24, 1874, February 12, 1880; Belgium, December 24, 1874; Luxembourg, March 9, 1876; Brazil, September 17, 1877; Spain, May 2, 1878.

Great Britain.

Denmark, April 15, 1862, March 31, 1873; Prussia, March 5, 1864; Belgium, July 31, 1872, May 20, 1876; Brazil, November 13, 1872; Italy, February 5, 1873, January 15, 1875; Sweden and Norway, June 26, 1873; Austria, December 3, 1873; Honduras, January 6, 1874; Prussia, March 5, 1874; Netherlands, June 19, 1874; Switzerland, November 28, 1874. December 3, 1878, December 8, 1879, November 26, 1880; Hayti, December 2, 1874; France, August 14, 1876; Spain, June 4, 1878; Portugal, March 8, 1879; Luxembourg, November 24, 1880; Salvador, June 23, 1881; Uruguay, March 26, 1884; Guatemala, July 4, 1885.

Greece.

Austria, March 28, 1874; Italy, November 17, 1877.

Italy.

Austria, February 27, 1869, March 30, 1875; Greece, February 27, 1869, March 30, 1875, November 17, 1877; Honduras, June 15, 1869; France, May 12, 1870, July 16, 1873; Peru, August 21, 1870, March 22, 1873; Mexico, December 17, 1870; Russia, May 13, 1871; Brazil, November 12, 1872; Great Britain, February 5, 1873, January 15, 1875; Costa Rica, March 6, 1873; Denmark, July 19, 1873; Germany, July 25, 1873; Switzerland, July 25, 1873; Belgium, January 15, 1875; Portugal, March 18, 1878; Uruguay, October 25, 1878, April 14, 1879; Roumania, August 23, 1880.

Luxembourg.

United States, October 29, 1883.

Montenegro.

Austria, September 23, 1872.

Netherlands.

Great Britain, June 19, 1874; France, September 12, 1875; Germany, March 9, 1876; Monaco, August 10, 1876; Belgium, January 16, 1877; Luxembourg, June 21, 1877; Denmark, July 28, 1877; Sweden and Norway, March 11, 1879; Austria, November 24, 1880, February 11, 1882, February 12, 1882; Brazil, June 1, 1881; Russia, August 13, 1883.

Portugal.

France, December 30, 1872; Belgium, March 8, 1875, December 16, 1881; Netherlands, March 3, 1878; Italy, March 18, 1878; Great Britain, August 6, 1879.

Roumania.

Belgium, August 15, 1880; Italy, August 23, 1880; Netherlands, September 13, 1881.

Russia.

Italy, May 13, 1871; Belgium, August 4, 1872, July 29, 1881; Switzerland, November 17, 1873; Austria, October 15, 1874; Spain, December 14, 1876; Netherlands, August 13, 1880; Monaco, September 5, 1883; Bavaria, September 19, 1885.

Servia.

Italy, November 9, 1879; Belgium, March 23, 1881; Austria, May 6, 1881.

Spain.

Belgium, June 17, 1870, January 28, 1876; United States, January 5, 1877; Russia, March 21, 1877; France, December 14, 1877; Germany, May 2, 1878; Great Britain, June 4, 1878; Netherlands, March 9, 1879; Monaco, April 6, 1882.

Sweden and Norway.

Great Britain, June 26, 1873; Germany, January 19, 1878; Italy, May 28, 1878; Netherlands, March 11, 1879.

Switzerland.

Italy, July 22, 1868; Germany, July 25, 1873, January 24, 1874; Italy, July 25, 1873; Belgium, May 13, 1874; Great Britain, November 28, 1874, December 8, 1879; Luxembourg, February 30, 1876; Portugal, October 30, 1877; Spain, August 31, 1883; Salvador, October 30, 1883.

Turkey.

United States, August 11, 1874.

AMERICAN STATES.

Brazil.

Paraguay, January 16, 1872; Great Britain, November 13, 1872; Germany, September 17, 1877; Netherlands, June 1, 1881.

Equador.

United States, June 28, 1872.

Guatemala.

Great Britain, July 4, 1885.

Honduras.

Italy, June 15, 1869.

Hayti.

Great Britain, December 7, 1874.

Mexico.

Italy, December 17, 1870; Belgium, May 12, 1881; United States, August 7, 1882.

Peru.

Italy, August 21, 1870, March 22, 1873; Belgium, August 14, 1874.

Salvador.

Belgium, February 27, 1880.

United States.

Salvador, May 23, 1870; Nicaragua, June 25, 1870; Peru, September 12, 1870; Equador, June 28, 1872; Belgium, March 19, 1874, June 13, 1882; Turkey, August 11, 1874; Spain, January 5, 1877; Netherlands, May 22, 1880; Mexico, August 7, 1882; Luxembourg, October 29, 1883.

Uruguay.

Italy, October 25, 1878, April 14, 1879; Germany, February 12, 1880; Great Britain, March 26, 1884

Venezuela.

Belgium, March 13, 1884.

CHAPTER XXII.

PRIVATE INTERNATIONAL LAW.

SECTION I.—NATURE OF PRIVATE INTERNATIONAL LAW.

373. PRIVATE international law consists of the principles and rules by which persons and things residing or situated in a country are affected by the laws prevailing in another.

374. Such rules may affect the status of the person, marriage and divorce, acts and contracts, corporeal and incorporeal property, successions, legal proceedings, foreign judgments, and the commission of crime.

SECTION II.—DOMICILE.

375. The national character of a person de-

pends on his domicile, which may be either of origin or of choice.

376. The domicile of origin is the place of birth or the native land; that of choice is the place of residence with an express or implied intention of dwelling in it.

377. A wife has the domicile of her husband, and a minor that of his parents.

378. The ambassador preserves the domicile of the country which he represents, but the consul, if he engages in trade, acquires the domicile of the place where he resides.

Section III.—Status.

379. Conflicting rules obtain as to the laws which should govern the status and capacity of the person. By the French and Italian rules the status and capacity of the persons are governed by the law of origin; by the British and American they are governed by the law of domicile.

Section IV.—Marriage.

380. A marriage valid according to the law of the place where it was contracted is valid everywhere. If invalid there it is invalid everywhere, and the issues of the same would be held illegitimate.

381. The *lex loci actus* governs the form and ceremonies of marriage, but there is a conflict of law as regards the need of the consent of parents and guardians and the capacity of the party to contract the same.

By the Italian Code, s. 102, the capacity of an alien to contract marriage is determined by the law of the country to which he belongs. An alien wishing to contract marriage in the kingdom must present to the officer of the Civil State a declaration from a competent authority in the country to which he belongs, showing that there is nothing contrary to such marriage in the laws by which he is governed.

Section V.—Acts and Contracts.

382. The validity of any act or contract is decided by the *lex loci contractus* or the law of the place where it is made.

383. All the formalities and proofs required by the law of the place where the contract is made are likewise indispensable for their validity everywhere else.

384. The law of the place where the contract is made governs also the interest and damages in a contract.

385. Every person contracting in a country is understood to submit himself to the law of the same, and to accept its action upon his contract.

386. In the interpretation of contracts the law and customs of the place where the contract was made to govern in all cases when the language is not directly expressive of the actual intention of the parties, and they are tacitly inferred from the nature, objects, and occasion of the contract.

387. The law of the place where the contract is to be executed or the *lex fori* regulates the remedies.

SECTION VI.—SUCCESSIONS.

388. The succession to movable property

of a person dying intestate is governed by the law of the place of domicile of the intestate at the time of his death.

389. A conflict of law exists on the power of the testator. Foreign law empowers him to adopt the form either required by the *lex loci actio* or by the *lex domicilii*. English law compels him to adopt the form prescribed by the *lex domicilii*.

390. The law of domicile governs the construction of the testamentary instrument, unless the testator expressly states that he had in view the *lex sitûs*.

391. The following treaties exist, regulating the reciprocal communication of acts relating to the status of the person, and also the administration of successions

SECTION VII.—TREATY CLAUSES CONCERNING THE ADMINISTRATION OF SUCCESSIONS.

See Treaties between Austria and France of January 5, 1879; Austria and Servia, May 6, 1881; Brazil and Italy, June 14, 1879; France and Russia, April 1, 1874; Germany and Russia, November 12,

1874; *Great Britain and Prussia, August* 9, 1880; *Italy and Russia, April* 28, 1875; *Spain and Russia, June* 26, 1876.

392. The declarations and sentences of power and recognition pronounced by competent judges in one of the two countries in favour of the heirs and legatees interested in successions opened in their absence in the other countries will be executed in the latter on their being for that purpose communicated by diplomatic means or presented by attorneys.

393. These declarations or sentences will indicate the degree of parentage of the heirs or the title of the legatees, in order that the tax due for the same may be assessed by the Treasuries of the two countries.

394. When these are communicated by diplomatic means, they must be accompanied by translations made by the Consul residing in the place where they are executed; and if they are presented by attorneys, they must be authenticated by the Consul residing in the country from which they are sent, and accompanied by a translation made in the place where they are executed,

whether by the Consul there established or by
sworn translators.

Section VIII.—Property.

395. Movable property is subject to the law
of the place where the owner resides. Land and
other immovable property are governed by the
law of the place where such property is situated.

396. Public funds and stocks, as well as
shares of bodies politic, corporate, or semi-
corporate, are governed by the law by which
they are created, subject to any restriction imposed by the law of the place where the same are
delivered or transferred.

397. Property in shipping is governed by the
municipal law which determines the nationality
of the vessel.

398. Incorporeal chattels, including rights or
interests which may grow out of or incident to
personal property, such as patent right, or the
exclusive privilege of selling and publishing
particular contrivances of art, trade mark, or
the exclusive privilege of a manufacturer to sell
goods under a certain mark or name, and copy-

right, or the exclusive privilege of the writer or his assignee of selling and publishing particular works of literature or designs, are all governed by the law of domicile.

SECTION IX.—CONFLICT OF PRIVATE INTERNATIONAL LAW.

Whilst Minister of Foreign Affairs of the Italian Government, Sig. Mancini, in September, 1881, opened communication with foreign Powers with a view to the settlement of certain rules, uniform in all States, relative to the civil condition of aliens, the extension and guarantee of their rights, and their participation in the benefits of their respective legislation. And in furtherance of the object he sent the following Memorandum :—

"I. Jurists and statesmen have noticed with regret the incontestable imperfection of international relations in what regards the civil condition of foreigners, the extension and guarantee of their rights, and their participation in the benefits of their respective legislation. Such a state of things is, unhappily, inevitable, so long as there is no system of fundamental laws accepted in common, and consented to by the Powers, of a nature to terminate the uncertainty inherent to the jurisprudence of each country under the influence of different legislation. A few examples will enable us to appreciate the extent of the inconvenience in question.

"II. In several countries of Europe the law which regulates the *status* and capacity of the person, or, in other terms, the *personal status*, is the *Lex domicilii;* that is to say, the law of the place where the person fixes his domicile or his principal establishment, without any regard to his nationality.

"The Code Napoleon, on the contrary, has the merit of being the first to make the personal status of the Frenchman depend on his national law, so as to cover him with its protection wherever he might go. This rational substitution of the principle of nationality for the accidental and empiric principle of domicile, necessarily variable, has been equally introduced in other modern legislations, and in the new Italian Civil Code.

"But these different rules produce an insoluble conflict between the legislation of the countries which make the civil status or capacity of the individual depend on the rules in force in the State where he has a domicile, and those which make such capacity depend on the nationality of origin.

"The same conflict affects a French or an Italian subject who may be born in England or South America, because whilst a South American, according to the law of his country, is deemed to have the nationality and to follow the civil condition of his father, English or Brazilian law considers the same person as English or Brazilian by the simple fact of his birth in the territory of these countries.

"A French or an Italian woman marrying an Englishman loses the personal status of origin in virtue of the law of his country; yet she might have acquired at the same time the personal status of her husband, because English law till recent years did not accord the right of English nationality to a foreign woman who married an Englishman.

"The loss of French or Italian nationality by one of the causes foreseen in their respective Codes, or the protection of French law accorded to an Italian, or, lastly, Italian naturalization accorded to a Frenchman, produce, according to the spirit of the legislation and jurisprudence of France, simple individual effects; that is, effects which do not extend to the wife or to the children the issue of the individual, such issue not being affected by what is exclusively of a personal character. And yet according to the Italian Civil Code this change of status applies also to the wife and children of the individual, who acquire the new nationality of their father. Here we have, then, an inextricable conflict between France and Italy, each of the two magistratures having to give to the same individuals a different nationality.

"III. If we pass to the region of property, it is easy to multiply examples of such contradictions. It is sufficient to state that on the subject of movable property the rule professed by the jurists, according to which *mobilia sequuntor personam*, receives in different countries a different sense and application;

thus some countries apply to movable property the *status personnel*, that is, the law in force in the place to which the owner belongs ; whilst others apply to it the law of the place of his present domicile, or by a juridical fiction the place in which they are deemed to exist.

" For what concerns *acts*, though the rule *locus regit actum* operates as regards their external form, great uncertainty exists as to what the law is which governs their substance.

" Lastly, as regards immovable successions, we are in the presence of two systems : whether to regulate successions according to the law of the country where the immovables are, in virtue of another juridical fiction, *tot hæreditates quo territoria ;* or to consider the right of succession as an emanation of the right of property, combined with the right of family, and submit consequently without distinction both movable and immovable succession to that same law, viz. the national law of the deceased, saving the exceptions and prohibitions which may exist in the law of public order of the territory where the immovables are situated, as in the case where these laws prohibit the creation of *fidei commis* and *main-morte*, etc.

" IV. The new Italian Code in its preliminary disposition has, it is true, substituted for tradition— more or less arbitrary and elastic—some fixed rules drawn up by myself in my position as reporter of the

under commission charged with this work. But
these rules are only obligatory on the Italian magis-
tracy, and it is clear that they cannot remove or
diminish the inconvenience and danger of the present
abnormal state of things, except by stipulating with
different countries one or more conventions to regulate specially this point, and to determine by an accord
more or less uniform, some precise rules which may
render the application to *persons*, things, and foreign
acts of one or other of the legislation in conflict.

"Some of these rules might be drawn from books
and reports of jurisprudence; and some are found in
special conventions, such as the abolition of the right
of *aubain*, the form of acts and testaments, hypothec,
and execution of foreign judgments. But the advantage of these accords, where they do exist, even
though they do not constitute a rational and complete
system, shows the benefits that would result from
conventions regulating and protecting the private
interests of international society. These rules, established on principles of justice, will give to the citizens
of the contracting States the largest enjoyment of
these benefits, and not allow cases to be decided from
considerations more or less accidental.

In a further memorandum, dated September, 1882,
Sig. Mancini adds: "Whilst respecting the independence of the legislative action of each country,
and leaving to each legislature the care of granting to
foreigners whatever treatment it may judge proper,

what is required is to agree on the mode of arriving at a uniform solution of matters beyond the province of national legislation. The question is of a character eminently international; it is not within the competence of any State in particular to settle; it belongs to the collective competency of such States as may desire to secure for the rights of their respective subjects due guarantee and protection. The formula is this : To determine, in cases where the legislation of different States is conflicting, what law shall be applicable on the persons, property, or acts of aliens ; to decide what shall be governed by national law, what by the law of the place of domicile, or what by the law of the place where the property is situated, or by the law of the place where the act was done.*

* " Négociations diplomatiques du Gouvernement Italien avec les différentes puissances relativement à la fixation par traité do certaine règles du droit international privé et à l'execution des juge. ments étrangers " (*Journal du Droit International Privé* (Paris, 1886), om. xiii. p. 1-11). See Documenti Diplomatici presentate alla Camera Dei Deputati, e Negoziati del Governo Italiano e convocazione di una Conferenza Diplomatica in Roma, 1885.

CHAPTER XXIII.

MEANS FOR THE PREVENTION OF WAR.

SECTION I.—GOOD OFFICES AND MEDIATION.

399. A RESORT to war may be prevented—

(1) By asking or accepting a third Power's good offices, with a view of conciliating the dispute ;

(2) By proposing or accepting the mediation of a third Power, and receiving at its hands proposals of settlement, retaining the power of accepting or rejecting the same ; or

(3) By leaving the dispute to arbitration.

400. By the offer of good offices the contending parties are brought to consider reasonably terms of conciliation, but the effect is not binding.

401. In the case of mediation the mediating Power is not a judge, but a friendly reconciler, and its intervention need not arrest preparations for war, and may not prevent ultimate resort to it.

402. At the Paris Congress of 1856, the Powers represented expressed a wish, in the name of their Governments, that States, between which any serious understanding might arise, should, before appealing to arms, have recourse, as far as circumstances might allow, to the good offices of a friendly Power.

403. And in the General Treaty of Peace (Art. VIII.) a clause was inserted to the effect that if there should arise between the Sublime Porte and one or more of the signing Powers any misunderstanding which might endanger the maintenance of their relations, the Sublime Porte, and each of such Powers, before having recourse to the use of force, shall afford the other contracting parties the opportunity of preventing such an extremity by means of their mediation.

Section II.—International Arbitration.

404. In order to avoid a resort to war States may submit their dispute to arbitration.

Numerous are the precedents of disputes settled by way of international arbitration. Among the Greeks the Amphictyonic League was in effect a tribunal of arbitration. Among the Romans the fecials had the same power. Cyrus, King of Persia, nominated the King of India arbitrator in a dispute between himself and the kingdom of Assyria. The Carthaginians, in order to avoid war, submitted their dispute with Masinissa to the King of Numidia for arbitration. A treaty of alliance concluded between the Argivi and the Lacedemonians had a clause, that if a difference should happen between the two countries, they would have recourse to the arbitration of a neutral state, according to the customs of their ancestors. In the Middle Ages the dukes of Perugia, Bologna, and Padua frequently acted as arbitrators. In 1298 Pope Boniface VIII. arbitrated between Philip le Bel and Edward I. of England. In 1319 Pope Leo X. arbitrated between Philip the Long and the Flemish. In 1783 a question of boundaries between England and the United States was left to arbitration. The Congress of Vienna of 1815 left several questions to arbitration, such as the debt on the Rhine octrois, the succession to the duchy of

Bouillon, the differences between the cantons of Ure and Tessin on the subject of custom-house and on a portion of the Dutch debt. In 1834–35 the King of Prussia arbitrated between France and England on the Portendic indemnity. In 1839 the Queen of England arbitrated between France and Mexico. In 1864 the Senate of Hamburg arbitrated between England and Peru. In 1869 the President of the United States arbitrated between England and Portugal. In 1861–72 the *Alabama* claims, by the United States against England, were settled by arbitration. In 1882 the claims of France and Italy against Chile for damages produced by her naval and military forces on their subjects were left to the arbitration of a mixed tribunal, consisting of persons nominated by the President of the French Republic (or by the King of Italy), the President of the Republic of Chile, and the Emperor of Brazil. In 1884 the claims of the United States against Hayti were left to the arbitration of the Hon. William Strong.

405. The submission to arbitration ought to be in writing, and the subject-matter submitted ought to be precisely formulated.

406. The contending parties may plead before the arbitrators.

407. Where several arbitrators are named

they must act together, and, in case of difference of opinion, the majority will rule the minority.

408. If the arbitrators are even in number and no agreement is obtained, the arbitration fails.

409. Power may be given to the arbitrators, in case of difference, to call in a third to act as umpire, and in that case his judgment is final.

410. The arbitrators so selected form a voluntary court of justice, and they have the right to adopt their own rules of procedure.

411. The decision once formally delivered cannot be reconsidered without a new agreement.

412. In an arbitration the contending parties commit their respective cases wholly and unreservedly to the appreciation and judgment of the arbitrators, and their decision is obligatory upon them unless the agreement to submit was insufficient, the arbitrators were morally incapable to act or have not acted in good faith, and unless the award was in excess of the reference or contrary to natural justice.

413. The award must be given within the time fixed in the submission.

414. The arbitrators must decide according to the principles of the existing International Law.

415. The Convention of Paris of 1873 (Art. XVIII.), for a Universal Postal Union, has a provision to the effect that in case of disagreement between two or more members of the Union as to the interpretation of the Convention, the question in dispute is to be decided by arbitration.

416. The declaration relative to freedom of trade in the Basin of the Congo (Art XII.) provides that, in case of serious disagreement originating on the subject of or in the limits of the territories, the Powers bind themselves, before appealing to arms, to have recourse to the mediation of one or more of the friendly Powers, and reserved to themselves the option of having recourse to arbitration.

417. In the protocol appended to the Treaty of Commerce and Navigation between Her Majesty

and the King of Italy, signed at Rome, June 15,
1883, it is provided as follows :—

Any controversies which may arise respecting
the interpretation or the execution of the present
Treaty, or the consequences of any violation
thereof, shall be submitted, when the means of
settling them directly by amicable agreement are
exhausted, to the decision of commissions of
arbitration, and the result of such arbitration
shall be binding upon both Governments.

The members of such commissions shall be
selected by the two Governments by common
consent, failing which, each of the parties shall
nominate an arbitrator, or an equal number of
arbitrators, and the arbitrators thus appointed
shall select an umpire.

The procedure of the arbitrators shall in each
case be determined by the contracting parties,
failing which, the commission of arbitration shall
be itself entitled to determine it beforehand.

The pact of union between Costa Rica, Guatemala,
Honduras, and Salvador, dated February 17, 1872, Art.
III., provides : The maintenance of peace between the
Central American Republics is a strict duty of their
respective Governments, and any differences which
may arise between them, whatever be the cause, will

be settled amicably by means of the mediation of the Governments which are not parties to the difference. In cases where the difference remains unsettled, the same shall be left to the arbitration either of the Central American authority which shall be afterwards established, or to the judgment of a tribunal of arbitration, composed of representatives of the neutral Central American Governments. The Government or Governments which shall infringe this principle will be guilty of treason against the Central American nations.

SECTION III.—PROPOSED COUNCIL AND TRIBUNAL OF INTERNATIONAL ARBITRATION.

418. In order to provide a readier means for the settlement of international disputes the following scheme for the establishment of a permanent Council of International Arbitration, with original and delegated authority, is submitted :—

419. Each State to nominate a given number of members, publicists and jurists, or other persons of high reputation and standing, to constitute a Council of International Arbitration.

420. Such Council may be held, as constituted, as soon as any two States concur in its

13

organization, and have nominated members for the same.

421. When duly organized by any number of States, the council will invite other States to nominate their members to the Council.

422. The Council will at its first meeting appoint its secretaries.

423. On the occurrence of any dispute between any States, the secretaries of the Council, at the request of any two members of the Council, shall summon a meeting to consider what steps may be adopted for immediately arresting any war measures already taken, or about to be taken, by the contending States, and for offering, if desirable, the aid of the Council in the way of mediation or arbitration.

424. When the contending States agree to leave their disputes to arbitration, the Council will appoint some of its members, and some other persons specially nominated by the contending States, to be a High Court of International Arbitration for the adjudication of the same, and its award in the case shall be binding on the contending States.

425. The appointment of the members of the High Court shall be made with special regard to the character and locality of the dispute, and shall terminate on the settlement of the dispute or abandonment of the arbitration.

426. It is not contemplated to provide for the exercise of physical force in order to secure reference to the Council, or to compel compliance with the award of the Council or Court when made. The authority of the Council and Court is moral, not physical.

427. Where, however, on the occurrence of any dispute the action of the Council is ignored by the contending States, it may be within the competency of the Council to consider the facts in dispute, and to report thereon to the States which it represents ; and likewise, when its award, on any dispute referred to it for arbitration, is set at nought, to communicate the facts of the case and its decision thereon to the same States.

428. The Council will make rules for its own conduct and for the procedure of the High Court of International Arbitration. The rules adopted in the Alabama Arbitration, and those proposed by

the Institute of International Law, may supply valuable suggestions in the framing of the same.

429. It is suggested that the seat of the Council shall be a neutral city, such as Berne or Brussels.

430. The appointment of members of Council should be for a definite number of years, provision being made for the appointment of new members to supply those who may cease to be members by retirement or death.

431. The members of Council, though appointed by the Governments, will not hold a representative character.

432. The cost of maintaining the Council shall be borne equally by every State concurring in its organization. The cost of any reference to arbitration shall be borne by the contending parties in equal shares.

Pierantoni, in his "Trattato di Diritto Internazionale," vol. i. p. 260, gives the following notes as regard the practice of International Arbitration in the Middle Ages :—

The arbitrators in the Middle Ages were mostly bishops or lawyers, because they were the depositaries of juridical science.   The bishops were at that time preferred, on account of the dignity of their character, and the frequency with which they had to settle controversies of canonical law.   The sovereigns chose lawyers, because they themselves were ignorant of the feudal or the Roman law.

From the sentence of the bishops, there was an appeal to the pope, on account of the spiritual jurisdiction which the popes exercised.

A security was often asked for the execution of the award.

If the award decided questions of property, the princes or cities simply accepted the same, or, to use the technical phrase, submitted to the award.

When the award ordered peace, the princes took note of the sentence, which was in effect a treaty of peace.

When the arbitrators were called to a place where a war was pending, the military forces, bound by the compromise, retired so as to leave the judges independent.

The inobservance of an accepted award became reason for war.

CHAPTER XXIV.

WAR AND ITS EFFECTS.

433. War is the exercise of force by one State against another, for the purpose of obtaining by coercion what could not be obtained by peaceful means.

" Le droit de la guerre dérive de la necessité et du juste rigide. Si ceux qui dirigent la conscience ou les conseils des Princes ne se tiennent pas là, tout est perdu ; et lorsqu'on se fondera sur des principes arbitraires, de gloire, de bienfaisance, d'utilité, des flots de sang monderont la terre."

434. War is defensive on the part of the State which only wishes to defend its rights, and offensive on the part of the State which intends to violate the rights of another.

435. The right to make war vests in the executive power of the State, with such limitations as the constitution may prescribe.

In the United Kingdom the right of making war and peace is vested exclusively in the Crown. The Crown, which declares general hostilities, can limit their operations; it can except individuals, grant particular passes, and exempt particular classes of the enemy's ships.

436. When a civil war assumes the character of a public war, and induces conditions affecting other countries, equal to those produced by public war, States thereby affected may find it necessary to accord to the contending parties belligerent rights.

The United States did not declare war against the Confederated States because they refused to recognize in the same any body politic as opposed to them, or capable of performing any functions of hostility, but claimed to disregard the insurrection as a rebellion of individuals risen to the dimensions of a war. They did in practice treat the rebels as belligerents, holding them as prisoners of war, making use of exchanges and other practices of war; but this was from necessity, to prevent retaliation, and from humanity. But they refused to recognize any authority in the Confederated States capable of even making a surrender, and neither the existence nor the disappearance of the Confederacy was noticed legally by the United States (Dana).

437. The presumed object of war being to cripple the enemy's commerce and to capture his property, a state of war implies a prohibition of commercial intercourse and correspondence with the inhabitants of the enemy's country. Therefore all such intercourse without the licence of the Crown is illegal.

Exposito v. *Bowden*, Exch. Ch., 7 E. and B. 763.

438. When a State declares war against another State, it is the same as if the entire nation should declare war against the other nation, and therefore all the subjects of the one become enemies to all the subjects of the other.

The principle is that every person belonging to a nation with whom a State is at war is an enemy; that war is declared not only against the Sovereign, but against every subject, women and children included. But surely this principle is untrue in actual practice. Women and children, the old and the sick, physicians and surgeons, who do not take arms, are not enemies. No modern nation make all the inhabitants of the enemy's country prisoners of war. War is now rather a duel between the military and naval forces of the States at war. Political interests may be at issue, but there need not be personal enmity.

439. A formal declaration of war is not necessary, but, when all efforts to prevent war are ended, the practice is to issue a manifesto within the territory of the State, announcing the commencement of hostilities and the motive for resorting to the same, which manifesto is communicated to all friendly Powers, and has the same effect as a declaration.

440. A declaration of war is an act of State done by virtue of the prerogative exclusively belonging to the Crown, and carries with it all the force of law.

441. War exists *de facto* as well as *de jure* after a declaration of hostilities has been duly made.

The Romans considered a formal declaration of war necessary to legalize hostilities between nations. A declaration of war continued to be made till the end of the seventeenth century. In 1635 a declaration of war by France against Spain was made by heralds-at-arms.

442. Knowledge of the existence of war is presumed to exist so as to affect even ships at sea, as soon as such public manifesto and accompanying orders, warnings, etc., have been issued.

443. The territory of the enemy includes all the place or region which is under his actual control, and of which he has firm possession, without reference to the political or legal relations of the territory to the general government, or to what Sovereign the territory which the enemy is holding belongs in time of peace.

"*The Alexander*," 7 Cranch, 169–179.

444. The national character of those living in the territory being determined by domicile, all persons residing and domiciled in the enemy's country are held as enemies, and subject to all the disabilities which affect the State.

445. The character of enemy does not attach to one whose residence in the place is of a mere temporary nature, or to one who resides there for diplomatic purposes.

446. The person and property of alien enemies or subjects of the country at war within the State are protected.

In England Magna Charta provided that merchants belonging to the country of the enemy, found in England at the breaking out of a war, should be attached, without harm of body or goods, until the king or his chief functionary be informed how our merchants are treated in the country with which we are at war, and if ours be secure in that country, they shall be secure in ours. It has been, moreover, held that when a foreigner is resident in England, and afterwards a war breaks out, his goods are not liable to be seized (Bro. Ab. tit. Propertie, 38 ; Forfeiture, 57).

447. War puts an end to all commerce and intercourse between belligerent States and the people within the same.

448. If a contract be made with a foreigner during peace the right of action upon it is not absolutely forfeited by the occurrence of a war, but suspended.

Steven's Commentary, vol. ii. p. 17.

449. Trading with the enemy being illegal, the property of the parties so engaged is liable to confiscation, and all contracts arising out of such trading are illegal.

450. A licence is necessary from the Government to legalize trade with an enemy's territory, as also to remove merchandise thence, even though the same had been acquired before the

war. The Sovereign alone has authority to grant a licence.

451. A licence never acts retrospectively. It permits to be done what could not be done without its permission.

452. Belligerent cruisers have the right to visit and search on the high sea any merchant vessel suspected of carrying contraband of war to the enemy.

453. The penalty for the contravention of the right of search is the confiscation of the property so withheld from it.

454. Belligerents have the right to capture all property belonging to the enemy, whether belonging to the State or its subjects, and all property subject to the ownership and control of persons domiciled in the enemy's territory.

455. Belligerent cruisers have the right to seize all contraband of war found on board neutral ships.

456. The captor is bound to bring the vessel and cargo captured to a convenient port for adjudication.

457. None but regularly commissioned ships of war have a right to make captures, or to exercise the right of search.

458. The Powers represented at the Congress of Paris of 1856 and parties to the declaration on maritime war, and those which subsequently acceded to the same, have laid down the principle that privateering is and remains abolished.

A privateer is a private ship, commissioned to assist in carrying on the war, and a ship so commissioned carries on board the commission or letter of marque. A ship which takes commissions from both belligerents is guilty of piracy.

459. A neutral vessel taking commissions from either belligerent and armed as a privateer departs from the status of neutrality.

460. All prizes belong to the State.

461. The object of the Prize Court is to suspend the property till condemnation; to punish every sort of misbehaviour in the captor; to restore instantly, if upon the most summary examination there does not appear a sufficient ground of seizure ; to condemn finally if the goods are prize

against any one, giving to all a fair opportunity of being heard.

462. Belligerents have also a right to blockade any fortified place or any portion of the coast of the enemy, but the declaration of maritime law declares—

463. A blockade, in order to be binding, must be effective; that is to say, maintained by a force sufficient really to prevent access to the coast of the enemy.

464. A blockade is a high act of sovereignty.

A blockade is a sort of circumvallation round a place, by which all foreign connections and correspondence, as far as human power can effect, are entirely cut off. In questions of blockade three things are to be observed: (1) the existence of an actual blockade; (2) the knowledge of the party; (3) some act of violation, either by going in or coming out with a cargo laden after the commencement of the blockade. The adequacy of the force to maintain the blockade is a question of fact or evidence. In the very nature of a complete blockade, it is implied that the besieging force can apply power to any point in the blockaded State. If the squadron be driven off by a superior force, there is a total defeasance of the

blockade and its operation. But the occasional escape
of small vessels on dark nights, or under other particular circumstances, from the vigilance of a competent blockading fleet would not evince that laxity
in the belligerent which amounts to the raising of
the blockade.

465. A siege is the circumvallation by armed
forces of an inland fortified place, as a blockade is
surrounding by a naval force of a maritime fort
or coast.

The object of a siege or a blockade being to force
the enemy into subjection, belligerents are thereby
led to use means of coercion of a most destructive
character, involving offensive and inoffensive people
alike, destroying temples and monuments, works of
art and public libraries.

466. A capitulation concluded by the com-
mander of the place and the chief of the army
on conditions expressly defined is binding as a
treaty upon both parties.

467. A blockade may be by notification or
by simple fact.

468. When it is by notification, the same
should indicate the precise limits of the blockade,
and the precise time of its commencement.

469. A blockade by simple fact ceases with the fact itself; when it is accompanied by public notification, the blockade is supposed to exist till it has been publicly withdrawn.

470. A breach of blockade subjects the vessel and all the property engaged in it to confiscation.

471. On the breaking out of war the Admiralty Court is clothed by the Crown with the authority of a Prize Court, such authority being limited to the continuance of that war.

472. The Prize Court is a Court of the Law of Nations.

473. In the United States of America the District and Circuit Courts possess all the powers of a Prize Court.

474. In France the *Conseil des Prises* take cognizance of all cases of prize.

475. By the Geneva Convention of August 22, 1864, modified in 1868, ambulances and military hospitals are to be regarded as neutral, and as such they are to be protected and respected by belligerents.

476. By a declaration signed at St. Petersburg, dated November 29, 1868, the signatory States bound themselves to renounce, in case of war among themselves, the employment by their military or naval troops of any projectile of a weight below 400 grammes, which is either explosive or charged with fulminating or inflammable substance.

477. No belligerent has a right to destroy the great features of nature, to choke up the avenues by which population communicate with the world without, and to deprive mariners of ports of refuge from the perils of the sea.

478. The end of war is peace.

CHAPTER XXV.

NEUTRALITY.

479. NEUTRALITY consists in abstinence from active interference in favour of either belligerent, and in a continuous adherence to impartiality towards them all.

During the American War of 1862–64, neutrality was designated as benevolent or malevolent. A nation exhibiting in her dealings sympathy and good-will towards both belligerents, and carefully abstaining from placing in the hands of either the means of injuring the other, would be held to practise a benevolent neutrality. A nation showing utter indifference at the success or failure of either belligerent, and putting in the hand of either every means of injuring the other, would be deemed to practise a malevolent neutrality.

480. A neutral must give no assistance to either belligerent, either in troops, arms, stores,

money, or counsel, and must not refuse to one party what he grants to the other.

481. A State has a right to preserve its neutrality in case of war between other States, and to remain neutral no declaration is required.

482. A neutral State has the right of continuing to hold friendly intercourse and trading with all the belligerents, and to carry on in time of war the trade which it was accustomed to possess in time of peace.

It was, however, held by the Prize Courts in England, in 1756, that a neutral has no right to carry on a trade during war which he never possessed in time of peace, especially a trade which might deliver a belligerent from the pressure of his enemy's hostilities. The rule of 1756 continued in force till 1798. (See 6 Rob. Rep., "*Wilhelmina*," p. 4. Also Orders in Council, 1806-7.)

483. A neutral State must not allow its country to become the theatre of strategic operation, must permit no recruiting of troops within its borders, nor allow any ship to arm in its ports.

484. Though permitted to continue to trade with both belligerents, the subjects or citizens of

a neutral State must not carry to either any article known as contraband of war.

485. Contraband of war consists of those articles which are in direct use in war, and of those also which, though in use in time of peace, may under special circumstances be declared contraband of war.

486. Of direct use for warlike purposes are arms, munitions of war, warlike stores, and military or naval officers ; also saltpetre, sulphur, gunpowder, etc.

Pitch and tar are articles of direct use in war, and are included as contraband of war. But they form the principal articles of industry in Sweden and Norway. A treaty was therefore concluded between Sweden and Holland, whereby these articles should be considered not as absolutely contraband, nor yet as entirely free and innocent, but as liable to the exercise of the right of war, that they should be subject to seizure for pre-emption (" *The Neptunus*," 6 Rob. Rep., p. 405).

Bynkershoek is in favour of not admitting as contraband those things which are of promiscuous use in peace and war (see Ortolan, vol. ii. p. 129). The following treaties were concluded since 1815, restricting contraband of war to arms and munitions of war, viz.:

United States and Republic of Colombia, October 3, 1824.

United States and Central America Federation, 1825.

Brazil and Prussia, July 9, 1827.

„   Hanseatic Towns, November 17, 1827.

„   Denmark, April 26, 1828.

Holland and Colombia Republic, May 1, 1828.

Prussia and Mexico, 1831.

Chile and United States, May 16, 1832.

France and Bolivian Republic, December 9, 1831.

„   Texas, September 25, 1839.

487. The carrying of despatches is contraband, and the conveyance of military persons subjects a ship to condemnation ("*The Orozembo*," 6 Rob., p. 433). The carrying of two or three cargoes of stores is necessarily an assistance of a limited nature; but in the transmission of despatches may be conveyed the entire plan of a campaign, that may defeat all the projects of the other belligerent in that quarter of the world ("*The Atalanta*," 6 Rob. Rep., p. 455).

488. The Maritime Law Declaration of 1856 laid down that neutral goods, with the exception of contraband of war, are not liable to capture under the enemy's flag.

489. A neutral must abstain from trading with

a blockaded port; but the Powers represented at the same Congress of 1856, laid down that the blockade to be binding must be effective; that is to say, maintained by a force sufficient really to prevent access to the blockaded port.

490. It would be a violation of International Law for the subjects of a neutral State to enter the military or naval service of either of the belligerent States as commissioned or non-commissioned officers or soldiers, or as sailors or mariners on board any ship or vessel to be employed as a ship of war of the contending parties.

491. It is likewise prohibited to neutrals to fit out, arm, or equip any ship or vessel to be employed as a ship of war, or privateer, or transport by either of the belligerent States; to break or to endeavour to break any blockade lawfully and actually established by or on behalf of either of the contending parties, or to carry officers, soldiers, despatches, arms, military stores or materials, or any article or articles considered or decreed to be contraband of war, according to the law and the modern usages of nations, for the use or service of either of the contending parties;

and all persons so offending incur and become liable to the several penalties and penal consequences of the statute law on the subject, and by the Law of Nations imposed or denounced.

492. The State is not responsible for the acts of its subjects. Its duty is performed when, on the occurrence of a war, the Sovereign, by proclamation or otherwise, warns the people against doing any act in derogation of the duties which devolve on neutrals, or in violation or contravention of the Law of Nations; and when it takes care to enforce its own laws concerning the matter (see s. 495).

In a despatch to Mr. Adams, the American Minister in London, dated December 19, 1862, Earl Russell, the Secretary of State for Foreign Affairs, stated that the Municipal Law of this country did not empower Her Majesty's Government to prohibit or interfere with the export of arms and munitions of war, except in extraordinary cases, when the Executive is armed with special powers; and that with regard to the Law of Nations, it was clear that the permission to export such articles was not contrary to that law, and that it afforded no just ground or complaint to a belligerent (Wheaton's "International Law," sixth edition, p. 571; Kent's "Commentaries," vol. i.). The President of the United States, in a message on December 31, 1855, said, " The laws of the United States do not forbid their citizens to sell to either of the belligerent Powers articles contraband of war, or take munition of war or soldiers on board their private ships for transportation ; and although in so doing the individual citizen exposes his property or person to some of the hazards of war, his acts do not involve any breach of national neutrality, nor of themselves implicate the Government " (" Correspondence with North America," November 3, 1863).

By the proclamation of neutrality issued in time of war Her Majesty warns her subjects that if any of them shall presume, in contempt of her royal proclamation and of her high displeasure, to do any acts in derogation of their duty as subjects of a neutral Sovereign in the contest, or in violation or contravention of the Law of Nations in that behalf, as, for example and more especially, by entering into the military or naval service of either of the said contending parties as commissioned or non-commissioned officers or soldiers, or as sailors or mariners on board any ship or vessel of either of the contending parties, or by fitting out, or arming, or equipping any ship or vessel to be employed as a ship of war, or privateer, or transport by either of the said contending parties, or by breaking or endeavouring to break any blockade lawfully and actually established by or on behalf of either of the contending parties, or by carrying officers, soldiers, despatches, arms, military stores or materials, or any article or articles considered or deemed to be contraband of war, according to the law of modern usage of nations, for the use or service of either of the contending parties, all persons so offending will incur and be liable to the several penalties and penal consequences by the Foreign Belligerent Act, or by the Law of Nations on that behalf, imposed or denounced. And Her Majesty further declares that all her subjects and persons entitled to her protection who might misconduct themselves on the premises would do so at their own peril and at their own wrong, and that they would in no wise obtain any protection from her against any liabilities or penal consequences, but would, on the contrary, incur her high displeasure by such conduct.

493. A neutral must not only abstain from taking any part in the hostilities, but must do nothing which may have the effect of hindering the operations of war permitted by the Law of Nations.

494. The Government of a neutral State is bound to do all in its power to hinder its subjects or citizens from violating the laws of neutrality.

495. The Powers represented at the Congress of Paris of 1856, and parties to the declaration

14

on maritime law, as well as those which have acceded to the same, laid down that the neutral flag is held to cover enemy's goods, with the exception of contraband of war.

496. By the Washington Treaty between the United Kingdom and the United States of America in 1870, the Government of a neutral State was declared bound *—

1st. To use due diligence to prevent the fitting out, arming, and equipping within its jurisdiction of any vessel which it has reasonable ground to believe is intended to cruise or to carry on war against a Power with which it is at peace, and also to use due diligence to prevent the departure from its jurisdiction of any vessel intended to cruise or carry on war as above, such vessel having been specially adapted, in whole or in part, within such jurisdiction to warlike use.

2nd. Nor to permit or suffer either bel-

* While assenting to these rules, Her Majesty's Government did not admit that they represented the principles of International Law in force at the time when the *Alabama* claims arose. They were accepted in order to evince the desire of Her Majesty's Government to strengthen the friendly relations between the two countries.

ligerent to make use of its ports or waters
as the base of naval operations against the
other, or for the purpose of the renewal
or augmentation of military supplies of
arms or the recruitment of men.

3rd. To exercise due diligence in its own
ports and waters, and as to all persons
within its jurisdiction, to prevent any
violation of the foregoing obligations and
duties.

497. The neutral State has a right to have its
territory and possessions, continental, insular,
and colonial, and all persons and property within
the same, respected by the belligerents.

498. The immunity of neutral territory in‐
cludes the prohibition of the passage of troops or
the harbouring of belligerent ships for purposes
of hostilities.

499. A neutral may allow a belligerent ship
to take refuge into its ports in case of storm.

APPENDIX.

THE SLAVE-TRADE.

DECLARATION OF THE POWERS ON THE ABOLITION OF THE
SLAVE-TRADE (TRAITE DES NÈGRES), VIENNA, FEBRU-
ARY 8, 1815.

"THE Plenipotentiaries of the Powers who signed the
Treaty of Paris of May 30, 1814, united in Conference,
having taken into consideration that the commerce known
as the African Slave-Trade has been held by just and
enlightened men of all times as repugnant to the principles
of humanity and universal morals ;

" That the special circumstances under which such
trade began, and the difficulty of stopping it suddenly, have
covered, to some extent, what was bad in it, but that at
last public voice has been raised in all civilized countries,
demanding that it should be suppressed as soon as possible ;

" That ever since the character and details of that trade
have been better known, and the evils of all kinds which
accompany it have been fully revealed, several European
Governments have taken steps to cause it to cease, and
that all the Powers possessing Colonies in different parts
of the world have in succession recognized, either by legislative Acts, or by Treaties and other formal engagements,

that they are under the obligation and necessity of abolishing it ;

"That by a separate article of the last Treaty of Paris, Great Britain and France bound themselves to unite their efforts at the Congress of Vienna to induce all Christian Powers to pronounce the universal and definitive abolition of the Slave-Trade ;

"That the Plenipotentiaries assembled at the Congress could not better honour their missions, fulfil their duties, and manifest the principles which guide their august Sovereigns, than in labouring to realize this engagement, and in proclaiming in the name of their Sovereigns the wish (*vœu*) to put an end to an evil which has for so long desolated Africa, degraded Europe, and afflicted humanity ;—

"The said Plenipotentiaries are agreed to deliberate upon the means for accomplishing an object so salutary by a solemn declaration of the principles which guided them in this labour.

"Consequently, being authorized in this act by the unanimous adhesion of their respective Courts to the principle laid down in the separate article of the Treaty of Paris, they declare in the face of Europe that, regarding the universal abolition of the Slave-Trade as a measure specially worthy of their attention, in conformity with the spirit of the age and the generous principles of their august Sovereigns, they are animated by the sincere desire of concurring in the execution of the shortest and most efficacious measure by every means in their power, and to act in the use of such means with all the zeal and all the perseverance which they owe to so great and beautiful a cause. Too well acquainted, however, with the sentiments of their Sovereigns not to foresee that, however honourable the object, they could only pursue it by just measures, having regard to the interest, habits, and the protection even of their subjects, the said Plenipotentiaries recognize at the same time that this general declaration could not prejudice the time which each Power in particular might regard as the most convenient definitely to abolish the Slave-Trade ; consequently the determination of the time when the trade shall universally cease will be the object of negotiation between the Powers; it being well understood that no means will be neglected to secure and accelerate the end; and that the reciprocal engagement contracted by the present declaration between the Sovereigns who have taken part in it, will not be considered as accomplished, but at the moment when a complete success shall have crowned their united efforts.

"In bringing this declaration to the cognizance of Europe and of all civilized nations on the earth, the said Plenipotentiaries hope to engage all the other Governments, and especially those who, by abolishing the Slave-Trade, have already manifested the same sentiments, to support them by their votes in a cause whose final triumph will be one of the most beautiful monuments of the age which has taken it up, and which shall have gloriously realized the same."

REGULATIONS ON THE FREE NAVIGATION OF RIVERS, 1815.

ARTICLES CONCERNING THE NAVIGATION OF RIVERS WHICH IN THEIR NAVIGABLE COURSE SEPARATE OR TRAVERSE DIFFERENT STATES.

"Art. I. Powers whose States are separated or traversed by the same navigable river bind themselves to regulate by a common accord all that pertains to that navigation. They shall nominate for that purpose Commissioners, who will meet at the latest six months after the end of the Congress, and who will take as their basis of their labours the following principles :—

"Art. II. The navigation in all the course of the rivers indicated in the preceding article, from the point whence each becomes navigable to its mouth, shall be entirely free, and shall not, for commercial purposes, be prohibited to any person, provided they conform themselves to the regulations which may be made for its police, in a uniform manner for all, and as favourable to the commerce of all nations as possible.

" Art. III. The system which will be established both for the perception of dues and for the maintenance of the police shall be, as far as can be made, the same for all the course of the river, and will extend, as well as special circumstances may not hinder it, to all the branches and confluents which in their navigable course separate or traverse different States.

"Art. IV. The navigation dues will be fixed in a uniform manner, invariable and independent of the different kind of merchandise transported, so as not to render a detailed examination of the cargo necessary, except in case of fraud or contravention. The amount of such dues, which in no case shall exceed those now in existence, shall be determined according to local circumstances, which does not allow the establishment of a general rule on this subject.

"Once the tariff has been regulated, it shall not be increased except by a common arrangement between the bordering States, nor, with the navigation, be burdened with any other duties than those fixed in the regulation.

"Art. V. The offices for the reception of dues, the number of which will be reduced as much as possible, will be fixed by the regulation, and no change will be made to the same except by common accord, unless one of the bordering States wishes to diminish the number of those which belong exclusively to itself.

"Art. VI. Each bordering State will charge itself with the maintenance of the towing-paths which pass by its territory, and with the necessary labour for the same extent in the bed of the river, so that there be no obstacle to the navigation.

"A future regulation will fix the manner in which the bordering States will concur in these labours, in cases where both rivers belong to different Governments.

"Art. VII. No forced stoppage or calling dues will be established. Those which already exist shall not remain, except when the bordering States, without regard to local interest, find them necessary or useful to navigation and commerce in general.

"Art. VIII. The custom-houses of the bordering States will have nothing to do with the navigation dues. Steps will be taken by special legislation to prevent custom-house officers putting any hinderance to navigation, but care will also be taken by the river police to prevent the inhabitants from carrying on any smuggling by the aid of boats.

"Art. IX. All that is indicated in the preceding articles will be regulated by a common agreement, which will also include whatever else may be necessary. The rules once determined shall not be changed except with the consent of all the bordering States, and they will take care to provide for its execution in the manner most convenient and adapted to circumstances and to the locality."

REGULATIONS ON THE RANK BETWEEN DIPLOMATIC AGENTS.

Signed at Vienna, March 19, 1815.

"To prevent the embarrassments which have presented themselves, and which may arise from the pretensions of precedency between the different Diplomatic Agents, the Plenipotentiaries of the Powers signatories of the Treaty of Vienna have agreed on the following articles, and they invite those of other crowned heads to adopt similar regulations:—

"Art. I. Diplomatic Agents are divided into three classes—

"That of Ambassadors, Legates, or Nuncios.

"That of Envoyés, Ministers, or others accredited with Sovereigns.

"That of Chargés d'Affaires accredited with Ministers of Foreign Affairs.

"Art. II. Ambassadors, Legates, or Nuncios have alone a representative character.

"Art. III. Diplomatists sent on extraordinary missions have not on that account any superiority of rank.

"Art. IV. Diplomatic employés will take rank among themselves in each class from the date of the official notification of their arrival.

"The present regulation will introduce no innovation relative to the representatives of the Pope.

"Art. V. A uniform mode will be settled for each State for the reception of Diplomatic employés of each class.

"Art. VI. Bonds of family or family alliance between the Courts give no rank to their Diplomatic Agents.

"It is the same as regards political alliances.

"Art. VII. In acts or treaties between several Powers which admit the alternative, the ballot will decide among Ministers the order to be followed in the signatories.

"The present regulation is inserted in the protocol of Plenipotentiaries of the eight signatory Powers to the Treaty of Paris on their sitting, March 19, 1815."

Here follow the signatures in alphabetical order.

DECLARATION RESPECTING MARITIME LAW.

SIGNED BY THE PLENIPOTENTIARIES OF GREAT BRITAIN, AUSTRIA, FRANCE, PRUSSIA, RUSSIA, SARDINIA, AND TURKEY, ASSEMBLED IN CONGRESS AT PARIS, APRIL, 1856.

"The Plenipotentiaries who signed the Treaty of Paris, March 30, 1856, assembled in conference,

"Considering—

"That Maritime Law in time of war has long been the subject of deplorable disputes;

"That the uncertainty of the law and of the duties in

such a matter gives rise to differences of opinion between neutrals and belligerents, which may occasion serious difficulties, and even conflicts;

"That it is consequently advantageous to establish a uniform doctrine on so important a point;

"That the Plenipotentiaries assembled in congress at Paris cannot better respond to the intentions by which their Governments are animated than by seeking to introduce into international relations fixed principles in this respect;—

"The above-mentioned Plenipotentiaries, being duly authorized, resolved to concert among themselves as to the means of attaining this object; and having come to an agreement, have adopted the following solemn declaration:—

"1. Privateering is, and remains, abolished.

"2. The neutral flag covers enemy's goods, with the exception of contraband of war.

"3. Neutral goods, with the exception of contraband of war, are not liable to capture under enemy's flag.

"4. Blockades, in order to be binding, must be effective; that is to say, maintained by a force sufficient really to prevent access to the coast of the enemy.

"The Governments of the undersigned Plenipotentiaries engage to bring the present Declaration to the knowledge of the States which have not taken part in the Congress of Paris, and to invite them to accede to it.

"Convinced that the maxims which they now proclaim cannot but be received with gratitude by the whole world, the undersigned Plenipotentiaries doubt not that the efforts of their Governments to obtain the general adoption thereof shall be crowned with full success.

"The present Declaration is not and shall not be binding, except between those Powers who have acceded or shall accede to it."

The Powers which acceded to the Declaration were Anhalt-Dessau, the Argentine Confederation, Baden, Bavaria, Belgium, Brazil, Bremen, Brunswick, Chile, Denmark, Equador, the German Confederation, Greece Guatemala, Hamburg, Hanover, Hayti, Holland, Lübeck, Mecklenburg-Schwerin, Mecklenburg-Strelitz, Modena, Nassau, New Granada, Oldenburg, Parma, Peru, Portugal, the Roman States, Saxe-Altenburg, Saxe-Coburg-Gotha, Saxe-Meinengen, Saxe-Weimar, Saxony, Sweden, Switzerland, the Two Hesse, the Two Sicilies, Tuscany, Uruguay, and Würtemburg.

When the Declaration was communicated by the French Minister, Count de Sartiges, to the United States of America, Mr. Secretary Marcy answered on July 28, 1856, that the United States would approve of the Declaration provided there were added to Art. I. the following words :—" And that the private property of the subjects or citizens of a belligerent on the high sea shall be exempted from seizure by public armed vessels of the other belligerent, except it be contraband." The Government of the United States also proposed to alter the form of the declaration into a Treaty on the subject. The consideration of the subject was, however, soon after suspended by the election of a new President of the United States (see M. Marcy's despatch to M. Sartiges, July 28, 1856).

THE TREATY OF WASHINGTON.

The Treaty between Her Majesty and the United States of America, signed at Washington, May 8, 1871, respecting the *Alabama* claims, provided as follows:—

" Art. I. Whereas differences have arisen between the Government of the United States and the Government of Her Britannic Majesty, and still exist, growing out of the acts committed by the several vessels which have given rise to the claims generically known as the *Alabama* claims:

" And whereas Her Britannic Majesty has authorized her High Commissioners and Plenipotentiaries to express, in a friendly spirit, the regret felt by Her Majesty's Government for the escape, under whatever circumstances, of the *Alabama* and other vessels from British ports, and for the depredations committed by those vessels:

" Now, in order to remove and adjust all complaints and claims on the part of the United States, and to provide for the speedy settlement of such claims, which are not admitted by Her Britannic Majesty's Government, the high contracting parties agree that all the said claims growing out of acts committed by the aforesaid vessels, and generically known as the *Alabama* claims, shall be referred to a Tribunal of Arbitration to be composed of five arbitrators to be appointed in the following manner, that is to say:—one shall be named by Her Britannic Majesty; one shall be named by the President of the United States; His Majesty the King of Italy shall be requested to name one; the President of the Swiss Confederation shall be requested to name one; and His Majesty the Emperor of Brazil shall be requested to name one.

"In case of the death, absence, or incapacity to serve of any or either of the said arbitrators, or in the event of either of the said arbitrators omitting, or declining, or ceasing to act as such, Her Britannic Majesty, or the President of the United States, or His Majesty the King of Italy, or the President of the Swiss Confederation, or His Majesty the Emperor of Brazil, as the case may be, may forthwith name another person to act as arbitrator in the place and stead of the arbitrator originally named by such head of a State.

"And in the event of the refusal or omission for two months after receipt of the request from either of the high contracting parties of His Majesty the King of Italy, or the President of the Swiss Confederation, or His Majesty the Emperor of Brazil, to name an arbitrator, either to fill the original appointment, or in the place of one who may have died, be absent, or incapacitated, or who may omit, decline, or from any cause cease to act as such arbitrator, His Majesty the King of Sweden and Norway shall be requested to name one or more persons, as the case may be, to act as such arbitrator or arbitrators.

"Art. II. The arbitrators shall meet at Geneva, in Switzerland, at the earliest convenient day after they shall have been named, and shall proceed impartially and carefully to examine and decide all questions that shall be laid before them on the part of the Governments of Her Britannic Majesty and the United States respectively. All questions considered by the tribunal, including the final award, shall be decided by a majority of all the arbitrators.

"Each of the high contracting parties shall also name one person to attend the tribunal as its agent, to represent it generally in all matters connected with the arbitration.

"Art. III. The written or printed case of each of the

two parties, accompanied by the documents, the official correspondence, and other evidence on which each relies, shall be delivered in duplicate to each of the arbitrators and to the agent of the other party as soon as may be after the organization of the tribunal, but within a period not exceeding six months from the date of the exchange of the ratification of this Treaty.

" Art. IV. Within four months after the delivery on both sides of the written or printed case, either party may, in like manner, deliver in duplicate to each of the said arbitrators, and to the agent of the other party, a counter-case and additional documents, correspondence, and evidence, in reply to the case, documents, correspondence, and evidence so presented by the other party.

" The arbitrators may, however, extend the time for delivering such counter-case, documents, correspondence, and evidence, when in their judgment it becomes necessary, in consequence of the distance of the place from which the evidence to be presented is to be procured.

" If in the case submitted to the arbitrators either party shall have specified or alluded to any report or document in its own exclusive possession without annexing a copy, such party shall be bound, if the other party thinks proper to apply for it, to furnish that party with a copy thereof; and either party may call upon the other, through the arbitrators, to produce the originals or certified copies of any papers adduced as evidence, giving in each instance such reasonable notice as the arbitrators may require.

" Art. V. It shall be the duty of the agent of each party, within two months after the expiration of the time limited for the delivery of the counter-case on both sides, to deliver in duplicate to each of the said arbitrators and to the agent of the other party a written or printed argument showing the points and referring to the evidence upon which his Government relies ; and the arbitrators may, if they desire further elucidation with regard to any point, require a written or printed statement or argument or oral argument by counsel upon it ; but in such case the other party shall be entitled to reply either orally or in writing, as the case may be.

" Art. VI. In deciding the matters submitted to the arbitrators they shall be governed by the following three rules, which are agreed upon by the high contracting parties as rules to be taken as applicable to the case, and by such principles of international law not inconsistent therewith as the arbitrators shall determine to have been applicable to the case :—

" *Rules.*

" A neutral Government is bound—

" First :—To use due diligence to prevent the fitting out, arming, or equipping, within its jurisdiction, of any vessel which it has reasonable ground to believe is intended to cruize or to carry on war against a Power with which it is at peace ; and also to use like diligence to prevent the departure from its jurisdiction of any vessel intended to cruize or carry on war as above, such vessel having been specially adapted, in whole or in part, within such jurisdiction, to warlike use.

" Secondly :—Not to permit or suffer either belligerent to make use of its ports or waters as the base of naval operations against the other, or for the purpose of the renewal or augmentation of military supplies or arms, or the recruitment of men.

" Thirdly :—To exercise due diligence in its own ports

and waters, and, as to all persons within its jurisdiction, to prevent any violation of the foregoing obligations and duties.

"Her Britannic Majesty has commanded her High Commissioners and Plenipotentiaries to declare that Her Majesty's Government cannot assent to the foregoing rules as a statement of principles of international law which were in force at the time when the claims mentioned in Art. I. arose, but that Her Majesty's Government, in order to evince its desire of strengthening the friendly relations between the two countries and of making satisfactory provision for the future, agrees that, in deciding the questions between the two countries arising out of those claims, the arbitrators should assume that Her Majesty's Government had undertaken to act upon the principles set forth in these rules.

"And the high contracting parties agree to observe these rules as between themselves in future, and to bring them to the knowledge of other maritime Powers and to invite them to accede to them.

"Art. VII. The decision of the tribunal shall, if possible, be made within three months from the close of the argument on both sides.

"It shall be made in writing and dated, and shall be signed by the arbitrators who may assent to it.

"The said tribunal shall first determine as to each vessel separately whether Great Britain has, by any act or omission, failed to fulfil any of the duties set forth in the foregoing three rules, or recognized by the principles of international law not inconsistent with such rules, and shall certify such fact as to each of the said vessels. In case the tribunal find that Great Britain has failed to fulfil any duty or duties as aforesaid, it may, if it think proper, proceed to award a sum in gross to be paid by Great Britain to the United States for all the claims referred to it; and in such case the gross sum so awarded shall be paid in coin by the Government of Great Britain to the Government of the United States at Washington within twelve months after the date of the award.

"The award shall be in duplicate, one copy whereof shall be delivered to the agent of Great Britain for his Government, and the other copy shall be delivered to the agent of the United States for his Government.

"Art. VIII. Each Government shall pay its own agent and provide for the proper remuneration of the counsel employed by it, and of the arbitrator appointed by it, and for the expense of preparing and submitting its case to the tribunal. All other expenses connected with the arbitration shall be defrayed by the two Governments in equal moieties.

"Art. IX. The arbitrators shall keep an accurate record of their proceedings, and may appoint and employ the necessary officers to assist them.

"Art. X. In case the tribunal finds that Great Britain has failed to fulfil any duty or duties as aforesaid, and does not award a sum in gross, the high contracting parties agree that a Board of Assessors shall be appointed to ascertain and determine what claims are valid, and what amount or amounts shall be paid by Great Britain to the United States on account of the liability arising from such failure as to each vessel, according to the extent of such liability as decided by the arbitrators.

"The Board of Assessors shall be constituted as follows :—One member thereof shall be named by Her Britannic Majesty, one member thereof shall be named by the President of the United States, and one member thereof shall be named by the representative at Washington of His Majesty the King of Italy; and in case of a vacancy happening from any cause, it shall be filled in the same manner in which the original appointment was made.

"As soon as possible after such nominations the Board of Assessors shall be organized in Washington, with power to hold their sittings there, or in New York, or in Boston. The members thereof shall severally subscribe a solemn declaration that they will impartially and carefully examine and decide, to the best of their judgment and according to justice and equity, all matters submitted to them, and shall forthwith proceed, under such rules and regulations as they may prescribe, to the investigation of the claims which shall be presented to them by the Government of the United States, and shall examine and decide upon them in such order and manner as they may think proper, but upon such evidence or information only as shall be furnished by or on behalf of the Governments of Great Britain and of the United States respectively. They shall be bound to hear on each separate claim, if required, one person on behalf of each Government as counsel or agent. A majority of the assessors in each case shall be sufficient for a decision.

"The decision of the assessors shall be given upon each claim in writing, and shall be signed by them respectively, and dated.

"Every claim shall be presented to the assessors within six months from the day of their first meeting; but they may, for good cause shown, extend the time for the presentation of any claim to a further period not exceeding three months.

" The assessors shall report to each Government, at or before the expiration of one year from the date of their first meeting, the amount of claims decided by them up to the date of such report; if further claims then remain undecided, they shall make a further report at or before the expiration of two years from the date of such first meeting; and in case any claims remain undetermined at that time, they shall make a final report within a further period of six months.

" The report or reports shall be made in duplicate, and one copy thereof shall be delivered to the representative of Her Britannic Majesty at Washington, and one copy thereof to the Secretary of State of the United States.

" All sums of money which may be awarded under this article shall be payable at Washington, in coin, within twelve months after the delivery of each report.

" The Board of Assessors may employ such clerks as they shall think necessary.

" The expenses of the Board of Assessors shall be borne equally by the two Governments, and paid from time to time, as may be found expedient, on the production of accounts certified by the board. The remuneration of the assessors shall also be paid by the two Governments in equal moieties in a similar manner.

" Art. XI. The high contracting parties engage to consider the result of the proceedings of the Tribunal of Arbitration and of the Board of Assessors, should such board be appointed, as a full, perfect, and final settlement of all the claims hereinbefore referred to; and further engage that every such claim, whether the same may or may not have been presented to the notice of, made, preferred, or laid before the tribunal or board, shall, from and after the conclusion of the proceedings of the tribunal or board, be considered and treated as finally settled, barred, and thenceforth inadmissible.

"Art. XII. The high contracting parties agree that all claims on the part of corporations, companies, or private individuals, citizens of the United States, upon the Government of Her Britannic Majesty, arising out of acts committed against the persons or property of citizens of the United States during the period between the 13th of April, 1861, and the 9th of April, 1865, inclusive, not being claims growing out of the acts of the vessels referred to in Art. I. of this Treaty; and all claims, with the like exception, on the part of corporations, companies, or private individuals, subjects of Her Britannic Majesty, upon the Government of the United States, arising out of acts committed against the persons or property of subjects of Her Britannic Majesty during the same period, which may have been presented to either Government for its interposition with the other, and which yet remain unsettled, as well as any other such claims which may be presented within the time specified in Art. XIV. of this Treaty, shall be referred to three commissioners, to be appointed in the following manner, that is to say :—One commissioner shall be named by Her Britannic Majesty, one by the President of the United States, and a third by Her Britannic Majesty and the President of the United States conjointly; and in case the third commissioner shall not have been so named within a period of three months from the date of the exchange of the ratifications of this Treaty, then the third commissioner shall be named by the representative at Washington of His Majesty the King of Spain.   In case of the death, absence, or incapacity of any commissioner, or in the event of any commissioner omitting or ceasing to act, the vacancy shall be filled in the manner hereinbefore provided for making the original appointment, the period of three months in case of such substitution being calculated from the date of the happening of the vacancy.

"The commissioners so named shall meet at Washington at the earliest convenient period after they have been respectively named; and shall, before proceeding to any business, make and subscribe a solemn declaration that they will impartially and carefully examine and decide, to the best of their judgment, and according to justice and equity, all such claims as shall be laid before them on the part of the Governments of Her Britannic Majesty, and of the United States, respectively; and such declaration shall be entered on the record of their proceedings.

"Art. XIII. The commissioners shall then forthwith proceed to the investigation of the claims which shall be presented to them. They shall investigate and decide such claims in such order and such manner as they may think proper, but upon such evidence of information only as shall be furnished by or on behalf of their respective Governments. They shall be bound to receive and consider all written documents or statements which may be presented to them by or on behalf of their respective Governments in support of, or in answer to, any claim; and to hear, if required, one person on each side, on behalf of each Government, as counsel or agent for such Government, on each and every separate claim. A majority of the commissioners shall be sufficient for an award in each case. The award shall be given upon each claim in writing, and shall be signed by the commissioners assenting to it. It shall be competent for each Government to name one person to attend the commissioners as its agent to present and support claims on its behalf, and to answer claims made upon it, and to represent it generally in all matters connected with the investigation and decision thereof.

" The high contracting parties hereby engage to consider the decision of the commissioners as absolutely final and conclusive upon each claim decided upon by them, and to give full effect to such decisions without any objection, evasion, or delay whatsoever.

" Art. XIV. Every claim shall be presented to the commissioners within six months from the day of their first meeting, unless in any case where reasons for delay shall be established to the satisfaction of the commissioners; and then, and in any such case, the period for presenting the claim may be extended by them to any time not exceeding three months longer.

" The commissioners shall be bound to examine and decide upon every claim within two years from the day of their first meeting. It shall be competent for the commissioners to decide in each case whether any claim has or has not been duly made, preferred, or laid before them, either wholly or to any and what extent, according to the true intent and meaning of this Treaty.

" Art. XV. All sums of money which may be awarded by the commissioners on account of any claim shall be paid by the one Government to the other, as the case may be, within twelve months after the date of the final award, without interest, and without any deduction save as specified in Art. XVI. of this Treaty.

" Art. XVI. The commissioners shall keep an accurate record, and correct minutes or notes of all their proceedings, with the dates thereof, and may appoint and employ a secretary, and any other necessary officer or officers, to assist them in the transaction of the business which may come before them.

" Each Government shall pay its own commissioner and agent or counsel. All other expenses shall be defrayed by the two Governments in equal moieties.

" The whole expenses of the commission, including contingent expenses, shall be defrayed by a ratable deduction on the amount of the sums awarded by the commissioners; provided always that such deduction shall not exceed the rate of five per cent. on the sums so awarded.

" Art. XVII. The high contracting parties engage to consider the result of the proceedings of this commission as a full, perfect, and final settlement of all such claims as are mentioned in Art. XII. of this Treaty upon either Government; and further engage that every such claim, whether or not the same have been presented to the notice of, made, preferred, or laid before the said commission, shall, from and after the conclusion of the proceedings of the said commission, be considered and treated as finally settled, barred, and thenceforth inadmissible.

" Art. XVIII. It is agreed by the high contracting parties that, in addition to the liberty secured to the United States' fishermen by the Convention between Great Britain and the United States, signed at London on the 20th day of October, 1818, of taking, curing, and drying fish on certain coasts of British North American Colonies therein defined, the inhabitants of the United States shall have, in common with the subjects of Her Britannic Majesty. the liberty, for the term of years mentioned in Art. XXXIII. of this Treaty, to take fish of every kind, except shell-fish, on the sea-coasts and shores, and in the bays, harbours, and creeks, of the provinces of

15

Quebec, Nova Scotia, and New Brunswick, and the colony of Prince Edward's Island, and of the several islands thereunto adjacent, without being restricted to any distance from the shore, with permission to land upon the said coasts and shores and islands, and also upon the Magdalen Islands, for the purpose of drying their nets and curing their fish ; provided that, in so doing, they do not interfere with the rights of private property, or with British fishermen, in the peaceable use of any part of the said coasts in their occupancy for the same purpose.

"It is understood that the above-mentioned liberty applies solely to the sea-fishery, and that the salmon and shad fisheries, and all other fisheries in rivers and the mouths of rivers, are hereby reserved exclusively for British fishermen.

"Art. XIX. It is agreed by the high contracting parties that British subjects shall have, in common with the citizens of the United States, the liberty, for the term of years mentioned in Art. XXXIII. of this Treaty, to take fish of every kind, except shell-fish, on the eastern sea-coasts and shores of the United States north of the thirty-ninth parallel of north latitude, and on the shores of the several islands thereunto adjacent, and in the bays, harbours, and creeks of the said sea-coasts and shores of the United States and of the said islands, without being restricted to any distance from the shore, with permission to land upon the said coasts of the United States and of the islands aforesaid, for the purpose of drying their nets and curing their fish ; provided that, in so doing, they do not interfere with the rights of private property, or with the fishermen of the United States, in the peaceable use of any part of the said coasts in their occupancy for the same purpose.

"It is understood that the above-mentioned liberty applies solely to the sea-fishery, and that salmon and shad fisheries, and all other fisheries in rivers and mouths of rivers, are hereby reserved exclusively for fishermen of the United States.

"Art. XX. It is agreed that the places designated by the commissioners appointed under the first article of the Treaty between Great Britain and the United States, concluded at Washington on the 5th of June, 1854, upon the coasts of Her Britannic Majesty's dominions and the United States, as places reserved from the common right of fishing under that Treaty, shall be regarded as in like manner reserved from the common right of fishing under the preceding articles. In case any question should arise between the Governments of her Britannic Majesty and of the United States as to the common right of fishing in places not thus designated as reserved, it is agreed that a commission shall be appointed to designate such places, and shall be constituted in the same manner, and have the same powers, duties, and authority as the commission appointed under the said first article of the Treaty of the 5th of June, 1854.

"Art. XXI. It is agreed that, for the term of years mentioned in Art. XXXIII. of this Treaty, fish oil and fish of all kinds (except fish of the inland lakes, and of the rivers falling into them, and except fish preserved in oil), being the produce of the fisheries of the Dominion of Canada, or of Prince Edward's Island, or of the United States, shall be admitted into each country, respectively, free of duty.

"Art. XXII. Inasmuch as it is asserted by the Government of Her Britannic Majesty that the privileges accorded to the citizens of the United States under Art.

XVIII. of this Treaty are of greater value than those accorded by Arts. XIX. and XXI. of this Treaty to the subjects of Her Britannic Majesty, and this assertion is not admitted by the Government of the United States; it is further agreed that commissioners shall be appointed to determine, having regard to the privileges accorded by the United States to the subjects of Her Britannic Majesty as stated in Arts. XIX. and XXI. of this Treaty, the amount of any compensation which, in their opinion, ought to be paid by the Government of the United States to the Government of Her Britannic Majesty in return for the privileges accorded to the citizens of the United States under Art. XVIII. of this Treaty; and that any sum of money which the said commissioners may so award shall be paid by the United States Government, in a gross sum, within twelve months after such award shall have been given.

"Art. XXIII. The commissioners referred to in the preceding Article shall be appointed in the following manner, that is to say:—One commissioner shall be named by Her Britannic Majesty, one by the President of the United States, and a third by Her Britannic Majesty and the President of the United States conjointly; and in case the third commissioner shall not have been so named within a period of three months from the date when this Article shall take effect, then the third commissioner shall be named by the representative at London of His Majesty the Emperor of Austria and King of Hungary. In case of the death, absence, or incapacity of any commissioner, or in the event of any commissioner omitting or ceasing to act, the vacancy shall be filled in the manner hereinbefore provided for making the original appointment, the period of three months in case of such substitution being calculated from the date of the happening of the vacancy.

" The commissioners so named shall meet in the city of Halifax, in the province of Nova Scotia, at the earliest convenient period after they have been respectively named, and shall, before proceeding to any business, make and subscribe a solemn declaration that they will impartially and carefully examine and decide the matters referred to them to the best of their judgment, and according to justice and equity; and such declaration shall be entered on the record of their proceedings.

" Each of the high contracting parties shall also name one person to attend the commission as its agent, to represent it generally in all matters connected with the commission.

" Art. XXIV. The proceedings shall be conducted in such order as the commissioners appointed under Arts. XXII. and XXIII. of this Treaty shall determine. They shall be bound to receive such oral or written testimony as either Government may present. If either party shall offer oral testimony, the other party shall have the right of cross-examination, under such rules as the commissioners shall prescribe.

" If in the case submitted to the commissioners either party shall have specified or alluded to any report or document in its own exclusive possession, without annexing a copy, such party shall be bound, if the other party thinks proper to apply for it, to furnish that party with a copy thereof; and either party may call upon the other, through the commissioners, to produce the originals or certified copies of any papers adduced as evidence, giving in each instance such reasonable notice as the Commissioners may require.

" The case on either side shall be closed within a period
of six months from the date of the organization of the
commission, and the commissioners shall be requested to
give their award as soon as possible thereafter. The
aforesaid period of six months may be extended for three
months in case of a vacancy occurring among the commissioners under the circumstances contemplated in
Art. XXIII. of this Treaty.

" Art. XXV. The commissioners shall keep an
accurate record and correct minutes or notes of all their
proceedings, with the dates thereof, and may appoint and
employ a secretary and any other necessary officer or
officers to assist them in the transaction of the business
which may come before them.

" Each of the high contracting parties shall pay its
own commissioner and agent or counsel; all other
expenses shall be defrayed by the two Governments in
equal moieties.

" Art. XXVI. The navigation of the river St. Lawrence, ascending and descending, from the forty-fifth
parallel of north latitude, where it ceases to form the
boundary between the two countries, from, to, and into
the sea, shall for ever remain free and open for the
purposes of commerce to the citizens of the United States,
subject to any laws and regulations of Great Britain, or
of the Dominion of Canada, not inconsistent with such
privilege of free navigation.

" The navigation of the rivers Yukon, Porcupine, and
Stikine, ascending and descending from, to, and into the
sea, shall for ever remain free and open for the purposes
of commerce to the subjects of Her Britannic Majesty
and to the citizens of the United States, subject to any
laws and regulations of either country within its own

territory, not inconsistent with such privilege of free navigation.

"Art. XXVII. The Government of Her Britannic Majesty engages to urge upon the Government of the Dominion of Canada to secure to the citizens of the United States the use of the Welland, St. Lawrence, and other canals in the Dominion on terms of equality with the inhabitants of the Dominion; and the Government of the United States engages that the subjects of Her Britannic Majesty shall enjoy the use of the St. Clair Flats Canal on terms of equality with the inhabitants of the United States, and further engages to urge upon the State Governments to secure to the subjects of Her Britannic Majesty the use of the several State canals connected with the navigation of the lakes or rivers traversed by or contiguous to the boundary line between the possessions of the high contracting parties, on terms of equality with the inhabitants of the United States.

"Art. XXVIII. The navigation of Lake Michigan shall also, for the term of years mentioned in Art. XXXIII. of this Treaty, be free and open for the purposes of commerce to the subjects of Her Britannic Majesty, subject to any laws and regulations of the United States or of the States bordering thereon not inconsistent with such privilege of free navigation.

"Art. XXIX. It is agreed that, for the term of years mentioned in Art. XXXIII. of this Treaty, goods, wares, or merchandise arriving at the ports of New York, Boston, and Portland, and any other ports in the United States which have been or may from time to time be specially designated by the President of the United States, and destined for Her Britannic Majesty's possessions in North America, may be entered at the proper custom-house and conveyed in transit, without the payment of duties, through the territory of the United States, under such rules, regulations, and conditions for the protection of the revenue as the Government of the United States may from time to time prescribe; and, under like rules, regulations, and conditions, goods, wares, or merchandise may be conveyed in transit, without the payment of duties, from such possessions through the territory of the United States for export from the said ports of the United States.

"It is further agreed that for the like period goods, wares, or merchandise arriving at any of the ports of Her Britannic Majesty's possessions in North America and destined for the United States may be entered at the proper custom-house and conveyed in transit, without the payment of duties, through the said possessions, under such rules and regulations, and conditions for the protection of the revenue, as the Governments of the said possessions may from time to time prescribe; and, under like rules, regulations, and conditions, goods, wares, or merchandise may be conveyed in transit, without payment of duties, from the United States through the said possessions to other places in the United States, or for export from ports in the said possessions.

"Art. XXX. It is agreed that, for the term of years mentioned in Art. XXXIII. of this Treaty, subjects of Her Britannic Majesty may carry in British vessels, without payment of duty, goods, wares, or merchandise from one port or place within the territory of the United States upon the St. Lawrence, the Great Lakes, and the rivers connecting the same, to another port or place within the territory of the United States as aforesaid: Provided, That a portion of such transportation is made

through the Dominion of Canada by land carriage and
in bond, under such rules and regulations as may be
agreed upon between the Government of Her Britannic
Majesty and the Government of the United States.

"Citizens of the United States may for the like period
carry in United States vessels, without payment of duty,
goods, wares, or merchandise from one port or place
within the possessions of Her Britannic Majesty in North
America, to another port or place within the said possessions: Provided, That a portion of such transportation
is made through the territory of the United States by
land carriage and in bond, under such rules and regulations as may be agreed upon between the Government
of Her Britannic Majesty and the Government of the
United States.

"The Government of the United States further engages
not to impose any export duties on goods, wares, or merchandise carried under this article through the territory
of the United States; and Her Majesty's Government
engages to urge the Parliament of the Dominion of
Canada and the Legislatures of the other colonies not
to impose any export duties on goods, wares, or merchandise carried under this Article; and the Government of
the United States may, in case such export duties are
imposed by the Dominion of Canada, suspend, during
the period that such duties are imposed, the right of
carrying granted under this article in favour of the
subjects of Her Britannic Majesty.

"The Government of the United States may suspend
the right of carrying granted in favour of the subjects
of Her Britannic Majesty under this article in case the
Dominion of Canada should at any time deprive the citizens of the United States of the use of the canals in the

said Dominion on terms of equality with the inhabitants of the Dominion, as provided in Art. XXVII.

"Art. XXXI. The Government of Her Britannic Majesty further engages to urge upon the Parliament of the Dominion of Canada and the Legislature of New Brunswick, that no export duty, or other duty, shall be levied on lumber or timber of any kind cut on that portion of the American territory in the State of Maine watered by the river St. John and its tributaries, and floated down that river to the sea, when the same is shipped to the United States from the province of New Brunswick. And, in case any such export or other duty continues to be levied after the expiration of one year from the date of the exchange of the ratifications of this Treaty, it is agreed that the Government of the United States may suspend the right of carrying hereinbefore granted under Art. XXX. of this Treaty for such period as such export or other duty may be levied.

"Art. XXXII. It is further agreed that the provisions and stipulations of Arts. XVIII. to XXV. of this Treaty, inclusive, shall extend to the colony of Newfoundland, so far as they are applicable. But if the Imperial Parliament, the Legislature of Newfoundland, or the Congress of the United States, shall not embrace the colony of Newfoundland in their laws enacted for carrying the foregoing articles into effect, then this article shall be of no effect; but the omission to make provision by law to give it effect, by either of the legislative bodies aforesaid, shall not in any way impair any other articles of this Treaty.

"Art. XXXIII. The foregoing Arts. XVIII. to XXV. inclusive, and Art. XXX. of this Treaty, shall take effect as soon as the laws required to carry them into operation

shall have been passed by the Imperial Parliament of
Great Britain, by the Parliament of Canada, and by the
Legislature of Prince Edward's Island on the one hand,
and by the Congress of the United States on the other.
Such assent having been given, the said articles shall
remain in force for the period of ten years from the date
at which they may come into operation, and further, until
the expiration of two years after either of the high contracting parties shall have given notice to the other of
its wish to terminate the same; each of the high contracting parties being at liberty to give such notice to
the other at the end of the said period of ten years or at
any time afterward.

"Art. XXXIV. Whereas it was stipulated by Art. I.
of the Treaty concluded at Washington on the 15th of
June, 1846, between Her Britannic Majesty and the
United States, that the line of boundary between the territories of Her Britannic Majesty and those of the United
States, from the point on the forty-ninth parallel of north
latitude up to which it had already been ascertained,
should be continued westward along the said parallel
of north latitude 'to the middle of the channel which
separates the continent from Vancouver's Island, and
thence southerly, through the middle of the said channel
and of Fuca Straits, to the Pacific Ocean;' and whereas
the commissioners appointed by the two high contracting parties to determine that portion of the boundary
which runs southerly through the middle of the channel
aforesaid were unable to agree upon the same; and
whereas the Government of Her Britannic Majesty claims
that such boundary line should, under the terms of the
Treaty above recited, be run through the Rosario Straits,
and the Government of the United States claims that it

should be run through the Canal de Haro, it is agreed that the respective claims of the Government of Her Britannic Majesty and of the Government of the United States shall be submitted to the arbitration and award of His Majesty the Emperor of Germany, who, having regard to the above-mentioned article of the said Treaty, shall decide thereupon, finally and without appeal, which of those claims is most in accordance with the true interpretation of the Treaty of June 15, 1846.

" Art. XXXV. The award of His Majesty the Emperor of Germany shall be considered as absolutely final and conclusive; and full effect shall be given to such award without any objection, evasion, or delay whatsoever Such decision shall be given in writing and dated; it shall be in whatsoever form His Majesty may choose to adopt; it shall be delivered to the representatives or other public agents of Great Britain and of the United States respectively, who may be actually at Berlin, and shall be considered as operative from the day of the date of the delivery thereof.

" Art. XXXVI. The written or printed case of each of the two parties, accompanied by the evidence offered in support of the same, shall be laid before His Majesty the Emperor of Germany within six months from the date of the exchange of the ratifications of this Treaty, and a copy of such case and evidence shall be communicated by each party to the other, through their respective representatives at Berlin.

" The high contracting parties may include in the evidence to be considered by the arbitrator, such documents, official correspondence, and other official or public statements bearing on the subject of the reference as they may consider necessary to the support of their respective cases.

"After the written or printed case shall have been communicated by each party to the other, each party shall have the power of drawing up and laying before the arbitrator a second and definitive statement, if it think fit to do so, in reply to the case of the other party so communicated, which definitive statement shall be so laid before the arbitrator, and also be mutually communicated in the same manner as aforesaid, by each party to the other, within six months from the date of laying the first statement of the case before the arbitrator.

"Art. XXXVII. If, in the case submitted to the arbitrator, either party shall specify or allude to any report or document in its own exclusive possession without annexing a copy, such party shall be bound, if the other party thinks proper to apply for it, to furnish that party with a copy thereof, and either party may call upon the other, through the arbitrator, to produce the originals or certified copies of any papers adduced as evidence, giving in each instance such reasonable notice as the arbitrator may require. And if the arbitrator should desire further elucidation or evidence with regard to any point contained in the statements laid before him, he shall be at liberty to require it from either party, and he shall be at liberty to hear one counsel or agent for each party, in relation to any matter, and at such time, and in such manner, as he may think fit.

"Art. XXXVIII. The representatives or other public agents of Great Britain and of the United States at Berlin respectively, shall be considered as the agents of their respective Governments to conduct their cases before the arbitrator, who shall be requested to address all his communications, and give all his notices, to such representatives or other public agents, who shall represent their respective Governments generally in all matters connected with the arbitration.

"Art. XXXIX. It shall be competent to the arbitrator to proceed in the said arbitration, and all matters relating thereto, as and when he shall see fit, either in person, or by a person or persons named by him for that purpose, either in the presence or absence of either or both agents, and either orally or by written discussion, or otherwise.

"Art. XL. The arbitrator may, if he think fit, appoint a secretary or clerk, for the purposes of the proposed arbitration, at such rate of remuneration as he shall think proper. This, and all other expenses of and connected with the said arbitration, shall be provided for as hereinafter stipulated.

"Art. XLI. The arbitrator shall be requested to deliver, together with his award, an account of all the costs and expenses which he may have been put to, in relation to this matter, which shall forthwith be repaid by the two Governments in equal moieties.

"Art. XLII. The arbitrator shall be requested to give his award in writing as early as convenient after the whole case on each side shall have been laid before him, and to deliver one copy thereof to each of the said agents.

"Art. XLIII. The present Treaty shall be duly ratified by Her Britannic Majesty, and by the President of the United States of America, by and with the advice and consent of the Senate thereof, and the ratifications shall be exchanged either at London or at Washington within six months from the date thereof, or earlier if possible.

"In faith whereof, we, the respective Plenipotentiaries,

have signed this Treaty, and have hereunder affixed our seals.

"Done in duplicate at Washington, the eighth day of May, in the year of Our Lord one thousand eight hundred and seventy-one.

(L.S.)	DE GREY & RIPON.
(L.S.)	STAFFORD H. NORTHCOTE.
(L.S.)	EDWD. THORNTON.
(L.S.)	JOHN A. MACDONALD.
(L.S.)	MONTAGUE BERNARD.
(L.S.)	HAMILTON FISH.
(L.S.)	ROBT. C. SCHENCK.
(L.S.)	SAMUEL NELSON.
(L.S.)	EBENEZER ROCKWOOD HOAR.
(L.S.)	GEO. H. WILLIAMS."

Note to page 63, end of paragraph on Suez Canal.

In March, 1885, an International Conference was held at Paris with representatives from Austria-Hungary, France, Germany, Great Britain, Italy, Russia, and Turkey, to make regulations for the free use of the Suez Canal, but no agreement was obtained. In October, 1887, a Treaty on the question was concluded between Great Britain and France, but the same has not yet been ratified, and will require the assent of the other powers.

INDEX.

16

THE END.

www.ingramcontent.com/pod-product-compliance
Lightning Source LLC
Chambersburg PA
CBHW021107270326
41929CB00009B/769